*Local girls know that white
men can give them more.
More excuses, more lies,
and more herpes.*

A

REVENGE
OF THE
SARONG PARTY GIRL

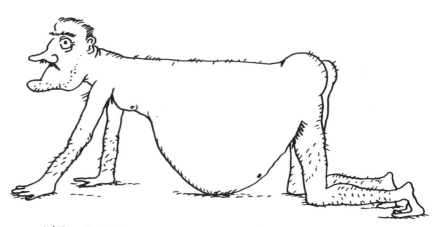

WHITE MAN - THE HUNTER

REVENGE OF THE SARONG PARTY GIRL

JIM **AITCHISON**

ILLUSTRATED BY

THESEUS **CHAN**

Angsana Books

SINGAPORE · KUALA LUMPUR

The persons referred to in this book are entirely fictitious. Caucasian males who don't know the meaning of this word should look on page 123 of Webster's New Dictionary.

Published by ❋ *Angsana Books*

Angsana Books is an imprint of
FLAME OF THE FOREST Pte Ltd
Yishun Industrial Park A
Blk 1003, #02-432
Singapore 768745
Tel: 7532071

Cover by Theseus Chan and Mangosteen Designs

Printed in Singapore

ISBN 981-3056-60-6

This is Jim after the SPG book.

And this is how Theseus looks now.

CONTENTS

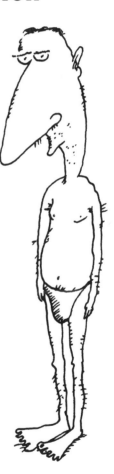

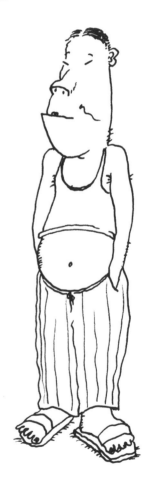

CHAPTER 1

THE FACTS

ABOUT

WHITE MEN

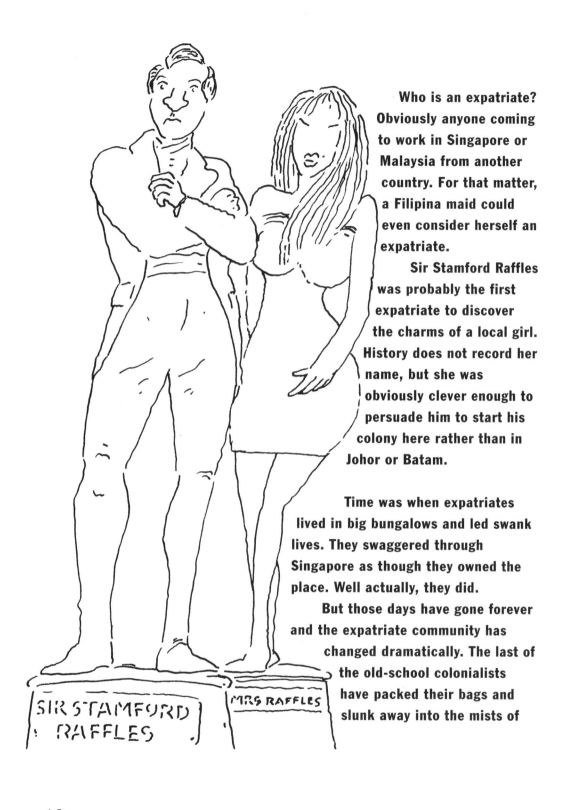

SIR STAMFORD RAFFLES

MRS RAFFLES

Who is an expatriate? Obviously anyone coming to work in Singapore or Malaysia from another country. For that matter, a Filipina maid could even consider herself an expatriate.

Sir Stamford Raffles was probably the first expatriate to discover the charms of a local girl. History does not record her name, but she was obviously clever enough to persuade him to start his colony here rather than in Johor or Batam.

Time was when expatriates lived in big bungalows and led swank lives. They swaggered through Singapore as though they owned the place. Well actually, they did.

But those days have gone forever and the expatriate community has changed dramatically. The last of the old-school colonialists have packed their bags and slunk away into the mists of time. Even ten years ago they were still in daily evidence: their safari suits a commonplace sight at the Tanglin Club.

Not any more.

Today's expat will be younger, more enlightened, without any preconceived ideas or prejudices. And, given the economic problems of the West, many are quite happy to work in Singapore or Malaysia on

ANG MOH IN SAFARI SUIT

local wages and conditions. They travel by bus or MRT, while more affluent Singaporeans speed by in expensive cars. They queue up at the hawker centres, while local businessmen luxuriate in five-star hotel restaurants.

They wash their own clothes and clean their own floors, while local families employ two or three maids to do the same work.

And, of course, today's expats mix more freely with their fellow Singaporeans and Malaysians. Instead of retreating to expatriate ghettoes, they'll be rubbing shoulders with your average Ah Hock. Chances are, they'll even marry his sister. Because the more people mingle, the more they close the door on malevolence.

In today's Singapore and Malaysia, unashamed and unshackled, locals can look newcomers in the eye and make their own decisions. Acceptance has to be earned, not taken for granted, and most expats know this. Should a Lim Chu Kang girl marry a London boy, or a Sydney girl marry a Subang boy, few eyebrows will be raised. A new maturity is at large.

But sometimes, old suspicions die slowly. Memories of colonial class differences and notions of racial superiority don't vanish overnight. A laugh or two can help them on their way. Because the more ridiculous prejudice is made to look, the less likely people are to uphold it.

AS THE CHINESE SAYING GOES... "LIKE CHICKEN & DUCK"

14

NOT USED TO OUR WEATHER, A JOG ROUND THE BLOCK
CAN TURN OUT LIKE A TRIP TO THE POOL

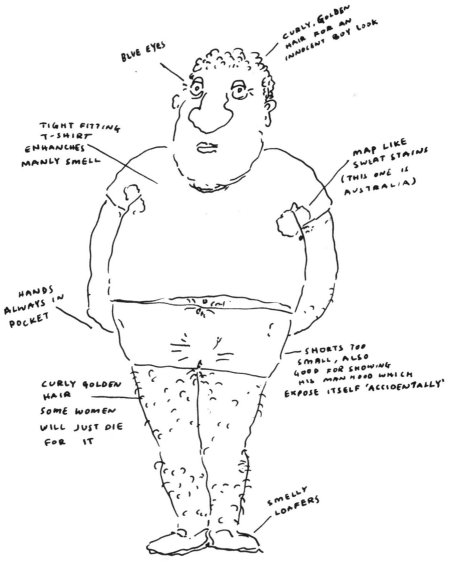

Supposedly, the red hair associated with white male Caucasians earned all expatriates the nickname of ang moh. The trouble is, most expatriates scouring Singapore and Malaysia in search of women have little or no hair at all.

99.4% of all Caucasian men consider that they possess Godlike physiques, charm and sexual prowess. What they do possess, in fact, are God-awful versions of the above.

A white man also believes that Singaporean girls are acrobats, ready to bend over backwards to please him. For their part, Singaporean girls think Caucasian men are from a circus, too: the freak show, possibly

A TYPICAL EXCITING ANG MOH EVENING

as The Elephant Man, with their organs growing out of their foreheads.

According to Singaporean girls, many white men exude a strange and unpleasant odour caused by their huge consumption of red meat. The pungency of the odour increases alarmingly with sexual arousal, and only diminishes upon gratification. Fortunately, this usually occurs very quickly.

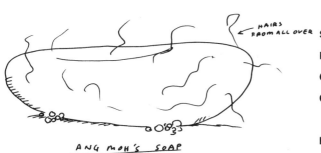

HAIRS FROM ALL OVER

ANG MOH'S SOAP

Many expatriate beds smell like bullpens, so many local girls fake a climax in order to go home early.

Over 50% of all white men have very hairy

EXPAT MEN OFTEN BOAST HOW LONG THEIR ZIPPERS ARE. THIS, OF COURSE SAYS A LOT ABOUT THE LENGTH OF THEIR PENIS. BECAUSE MOST OF THEM DON'T WEAR UNDIES, MANY HAVE BEEN CIRCUMCISED

ACCIDENTALLY.

YKK

bodies, the men especially. The more hair they have, the better: their bodies remain less visible.

The saucer-shaped depression in a white man's stomach is, of course, his navel. However, because his belly expands by over 48% after the age of 36, and by a further 88% after he turns 45, he can provide a Singaporean girl with an ideal resting place for her ear rings, or (depending on his age) an excellent depository for her shoes, handphone and purse. In extreme cases, expatriate navels can be used as a foot bath.

99.9% of all Caucasians believe they are highly astute businessmen, whereas 100% of all local businessmen know they're not. Caucasians happily pay GST (General Skin Tax) as a result of CPF (Caucasian Price Fixed).

Contrary to popular belief, the average Caucasian does not live a highly glamorous lifestyle. Most nights he will be home alone, watching TV and fantasizing over the female newsreaders. When his phone rings, it is mostly a wrong number. His biggest thrill each night will be soaking his white shirt and actually removing some of the stains. He will either cook his own dinner (usually Fish Fingers from Cold

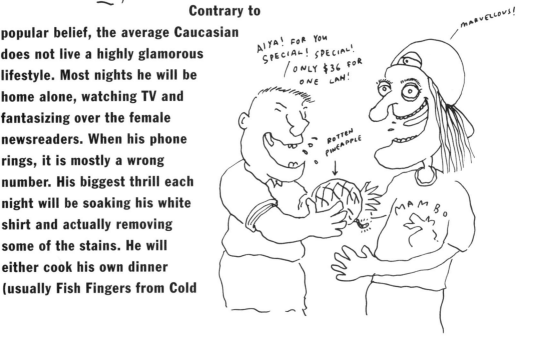

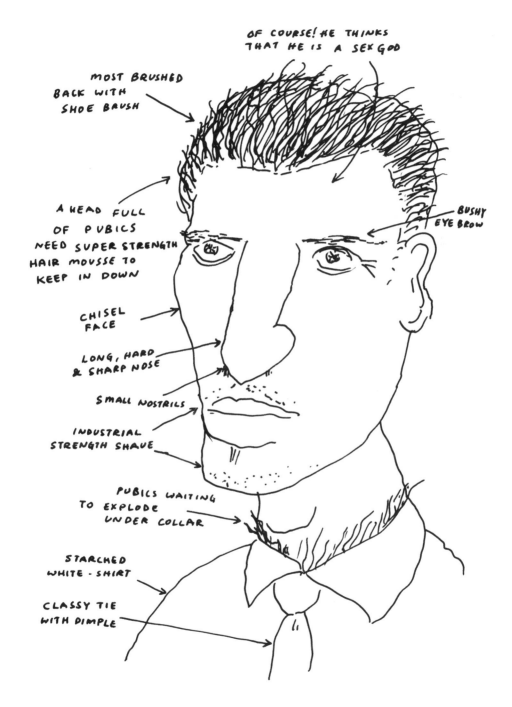

OF COURSE! HE THINKS THAT HE IS A SEX GOD

MOST BRUSHED BACK WITH SHOE BRUSH

A HEAD FULL OF PUBICS NEED SUPER STRENGTH HAIR MOUSSE TO KEEP IN DOWN

BUSHY EYE BROW

CHISEL FACE

LONG, HARD & SHARP NOSE

SMALL NOSTRILS

INDUSTRIAL STRENGTH SHAVE

PUBICS WAITING TO EXPLODE UNDER COLLAR

STARCHED WHITE - SHIRT

CLASSY TIE WITH DIMPLE

Storage, because he is too self-conscious to shop at NTUC Fairprice) or he will eat alone at a posh restaurant like Ponderosa or Long John Silver's.

On weekends he may have enough money to take home a bar girl. If he goes to the beach, he will probably be propositioned by a gay boy.

ANG MOH'S FAVOURITE BREAD

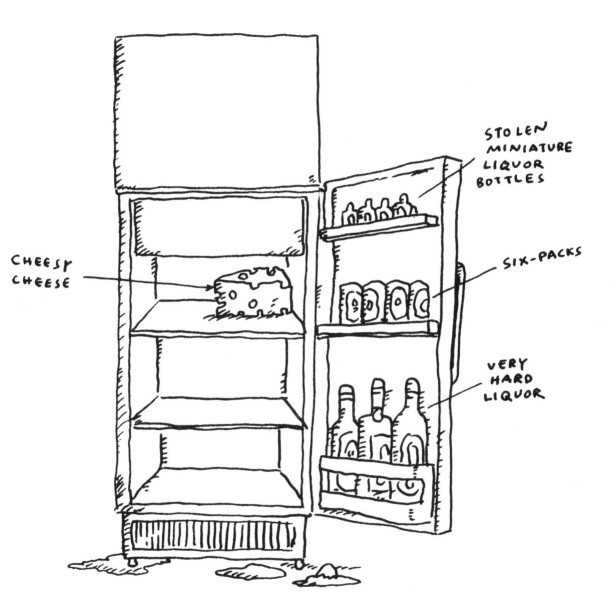

STOLEN
MINIATURE
LIQUOR
BOTTLES

SIX-PACKS

VERY
HARD
LIQUOR

CHEESY
CHEESE

ANG MOH'S FRIDGE

49.7% of white men do not know the difference between a lie and the truth. He usually begins by lying about

(1) his name,

(2) his address,

(3) his age,

(4) his marital status,

(5) his size.

PHOTO FOUND IN ANG MOH'S WALLET. USUALLY USE TO CHARM LOCAL GIRLS

In fact, 93.7% of white men have a phobia about the length of their organs. Six inches is regarded as the minimum acceptable length of manhood. This is because their bellies poke out so far, it is incumbent upon their organs to poke out even further.

Are white men more generously endowed than local men? According to Singaporean girls, about the only thing an expatriate is good at extending is his credit limit. Caucasian men appear to need constant reassurance that their organs are significantly longer. The shorter the organ, the more reassurance he needs.

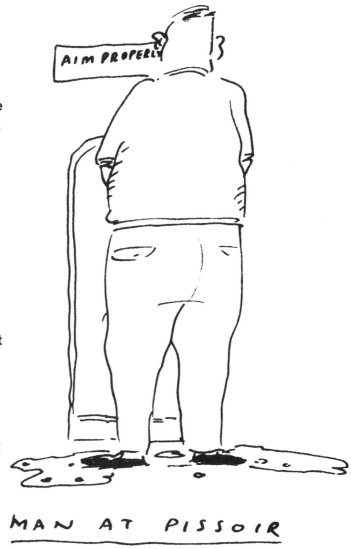

MAN AT PISSOIR

Being polite and not wishing to offend, Singaporean girls tell Caucasians exactly what they want to hear, even though the reverse is usually the truth, thereby perpetuating the myth.

So it seems that the local phrase 'Ang moh tuah kee' (White Man Big Thing) is not only offensive, but also inaccurate.

For their part, the ang mohs believe that eating red meat will boost their sex drives and add extra inches where they are needed most. Problem is, eating a truckload of rump steak usually adds inches in only one place.

A heavy diet of dairy products like cheese and milk is another favourite way for Caucasians to give their hormones a handy lift.

In fact, some ang mohs use any excuse to consume milk. One Australian called John pours milk over anyone he happens to wake up with.

BE CAREFUL WITH THE BEEF

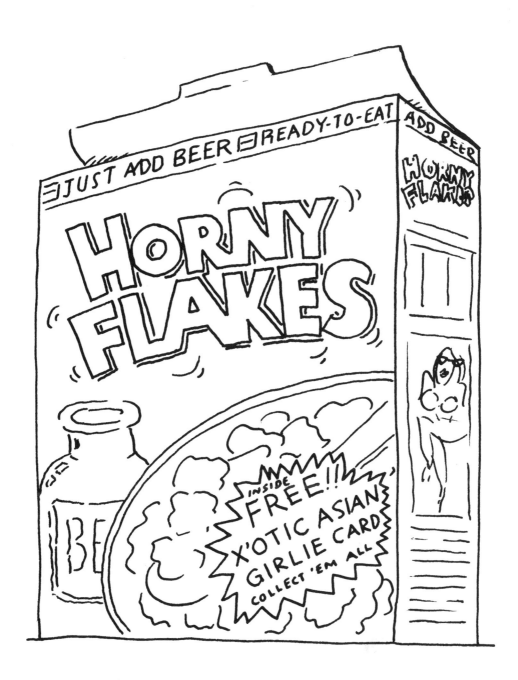

HOW ANG MOH START THE DAY.

As a public service to readers, here is the official International Rating of Male Organ Lengths on a scale of 10 to 1:

10   African Americans,
9   Melanesian Islanders,
8   Peruvian Bricklayers,
7   Asian males,
6   Mexican Tennis Players,
5   Japanese Sumo Wrestlers,
4   Fijian Bartenders,
3   Baby Mexican Tennis Players,
2   Argentinian Dwarfs,
1   Caucasian Expatriates.

Even more confusion surrounds the proudest part of the expatriate anatomy. Caucasian men are fond of giving names to the appendage which droops even lower than their beer bellies. As a result, some Singaporean virgins have concluded that Caucasian men possess two organs: one called William, the other called Richard.

POLYESTER COTTON Like expatriate men, it always comes pre-shrunk.

A CERTAIN DIGNIFIED GENTLEMAN.

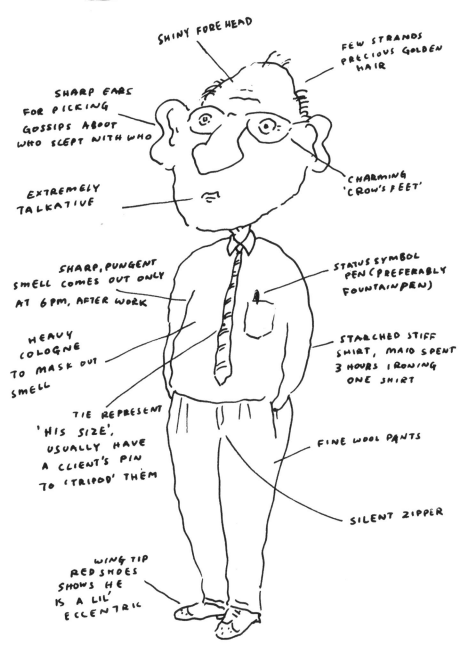

SHINY FOREHEAD

FEW STRANDS PRECIOUS GOLDEN HAIR

SHARP EARS FOR PICKING GOSSIPS ABOOT WHO SLEPT WITH WHO

CHARMING 'CROW'S FEET'

EXTREMELY TALKATIVE

SHARP, PUNGENT SMELL COMES OUT ONLY AT 6PM, AFTER WORK

STATUS SYMBOL PEN (PREFERABLY FOUNTAIN PEN)

HEAVY COLOGNE TO MASK OUT SMELL

STARCHED STIFF SHIRT, MAID SPENT 3 HOURS IRONING ONE SHIRT

TIE REPRESENT 'HIS SIZE', USUALLY HAVE A CLIENT'S PIN TO 'TRIPOD' THEM

FINE WOOL PANTS

SILENT ZIPPER

WING TIP RED SHOES SHOWS HE IS A LIL' ECCENTRIC

According to ang moh legends, a man's nose is the best indicator of his length. Big nose, tuah kee; well, so the theory goes.

Having a large nose can, of course, be an advantage. If nothing else rises to the occasion, a girl will always have something to fall back on.

STIFF
UPPER
LIP

CHAPTER 2

THE ANG MOH

SPECIES:

MYTH & REALITY

Singapore is the crossroads of the world, which probably explains why it's having a cultural traffic jam.

You see, while the Chinese, Arabs and Indians were the first waves of immigrants to descend on Singaporean shores, they are now being hotly pursued by a fourth wave: the white man.

And, while most expatriates think that all Asians look the same, it seems that most Asians think all expatriates look the same, too.

Therefore it is important to understand the cultural differences of the ang moh species.

The Australians aren't the same as the Americans. The British aren't the same as the Belgians. And nobody is the same as the New Zealanders.

What's more, not all ang mohs think the same. Not all ang mohs even think.

Ang moh men aren't always tall and handsome. Some are short and round.

Ang moh women aren't always tall and blonde. Some are short and round and black.

Some are even beautiful.

THE WIZARDS FROM OZ

Australia is a source of especially cultured men who revel in booze and talking to the boys. They spend so much time telling their friends how good they are at sex, they're usually too late to get any.

89.5% of Aussie men ejaculate very quickly. This is so they can run up to the nearest bar and tell their mates about it.

91.3% of Aussie men suffer from amnesia. This explains why they forget their manners, their addresses and their underpants.

92% also suffer from dyslexia, which explains why they always travel by NTUC Comfort taxis.

(Some are even dyslexic agnostic insomniacs, and lie awake at night wondering if there's a Dog.)

Many oversexed Australian expatriates have wrongly been called lechers. Actually, lecher is a common Australian word used in such phrases as: "Lecher hair down, luv" and "You go on top and I'll lecher know what it feels like".

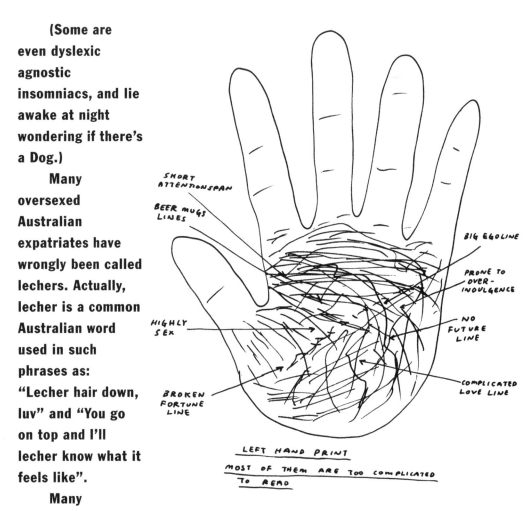

SHORT ATTENTIONSPAN

BEER mugs LINES

BIG EGOLINE

PRONE TO OVER-INDULGENCE

HIGHLY SEX

NO FUTURE LINE

BROKEN FORTUNE LINE

COMPLICATED LOVE LINE

LEFT HAND PRINT
MOST OF THEM ARE TOO COMPLICATED TO READ

Many Singaporean women believe that 93% of all Australian expatriates are called John. According to legend, only one of them is called John, but he's slept with 93% of all Singaporean women.

Australian men are the most resourceful men in the world. This explains why they invented the word "wanker", and have extremely smooth palms on their right hands. It also explains why they buy more soap than any other men in Singapore.

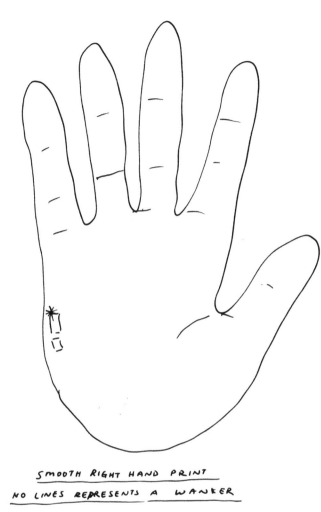

SMOOTH RIGHT HAND PRINT
NO LINES REPRESENTS A WANKER

Not all Australian men are interested in women. Over half the visitors to Desker Road are believed to be Aussie airline stewards. In a recent survey comparing the Eiffel Tower with Qantas stewards, it was discovered that not everyone had been up the Eiffel Tower.

Australian men have unusual hobbies. Some sniff bicycle seats in their spare time; others build condoms out of old toilet rolls.

Throwing up is a sign of manhood amongst Australian expatriates. In fact, the more they can drink, the more they can throw up. Throwing up in front of an Asian girl demonstrates intelligence and sexual ability.

The most commonly used Australian expressions to describe throwing up are:

Chunder,
Laugh on the grass,
Technicolor yawn,
Making a pavement pizza,
Having a Hoik,

Having a Ruth (R-u-u-u-u-u-th),

Having a Ralph (R-a-a-a-a-a-a-a-lph).

Australian expatriates also use very polite, discreet language to describe their bodily functions. Should an Australian man wish to urinate, he

THROWING UP OFTEN DEMONSTRATES INTELLIGENCE AND SEXUAL ABILITY

will announce that he is going to shake hands with his wife's best friend, siphon the python, or shake the dew off the leaf. He might also say that he is going for a snake's hiss or that he is going to Point Percy (at the porcelain).

When Australian men urinate, Asian girls often accuse them of aiming everywhere except the bowl. What she forgets, of course, is that Australia is a very dry country and needs all the moisture it can get.

Only an Australian man could go to the toilet in order to manufacture a Steaming Grogan.

On the whole, Australian men have a deeply sensitive attitude towards Asia. There is absolutely no truth in the news reports that the Australian Prime Minister once called his Malaysian counterpart a recalcitrant. The word contains far too many syllables for any Australian politician to remember.

TYPICAL AUZZIE JOKE

Q: WHAT'S SMALLER THAN A MOZZIE'S COZZIE?
A: AN ANT'S PANTS.

Australian men also have highly respectful attitudes towards the female body. The most private part of a woman's anatomy is known as her "growler", possibly because it reminds them of a tenacious little wire-haired terrier. Australian men, being highly considerate individuals, often keep a few cans of dog food under the bed in case the growler gets hungry at night.

TRUE BLUE BRITS

As the former colonial masters of Singapore, British expatriates believe they have a distinct advantage over other nationalities in the pursuit of local girls.

Many Englishmen believe they can attract Singaporean women simply by lifting their little fingers. What they don't realise is that when they lift their little fingers, many Singaporean women think they are having an erection.

BELCH The most significant contribution to any conversation which an Australian expatriate can make.

The British are famous for having stiff upper lips. However, Singaporean girls wish that other parts of their bodies were equally as stiff.

When a British expatriate asks a Singaporean girl for a quickie, it is one of the rare occasions when he is actually being honest.

British expatriates gain a lot from working in

SLEEPING WITH AN ENGLISHMAN

Singapore. They learn how to bathe more than once a week. And they learn that sleeping with a woman involves more than just sleeping.

Of course, many Singaporean girls prefer going to bed with an Englishman. At least she knows she will get a good night's rest. If she happens to be an insomniac, she can always lie awake all night and listen to his arteries harden.

Because British women rarely move or react during sexual intercourse, many British expatriates are totally unprepared for Asian women. When an Asian woman responds with wild abandon, she can expect her British partner to ask such questions as: "Sorry, luv, did I hurt you then?"

Like their Australian counterparts, British men have many highly intellectual ways to describe sexual intercourse:

Dipping the wick,

Giving work to the employed,

Taking the ferret for a run,
Driving the Porky Bus to Tuna Town.

These expressions are not intended to be crude; they merely reflect the British reluctance to call a spade a spade when it comes to sex.

In fact, many British men are so concerned about their sex drives that they seek medical advice to have them lowered. Their sex drives, of course, are all in their minds, which is precisely why they want them lowered.

Sadly, 82.4% of all British expatriates have slept with a transvestite. Apart from saving money, lonely British men are quite accustomed to having people turn their backs on them.

THE WELSH AND THE SCOTS

Every Welshman thinks he is Tom Jones and is quite likely to break out singing immediately he has reached a climax. He breaks out singing on many other occasions, too, such as when he washes his dog. (His dog, of course, will not be as hairy as him.)

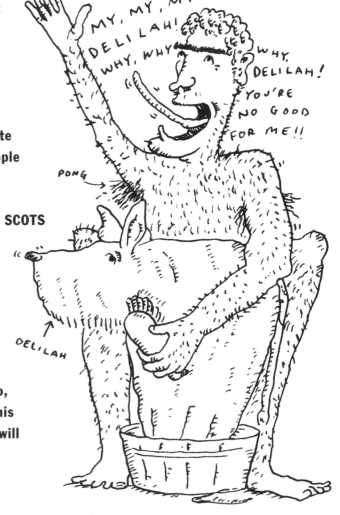

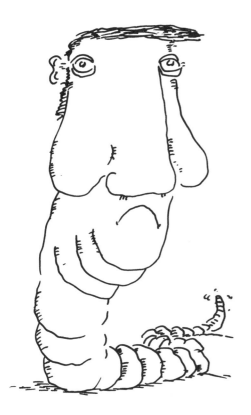

ROTI PRATA *Like expatriate men, they are round, tasteless and get cold quickly.*

Scotsmen, on the other hand, are more secretive and conceal their genitalia beneath a tartan skirt. Singaporean girls are often confused as to which clan a Scotsman actually belongs. All she has to do is lift up his kilt; if he has a quarter-pounder lurking beneath it, he is obviously a McDonald.

100% MEAT - QUARTER POUNDER

THE KIWIS

New Zealand expatriates have absolutely no interest in local women. Even in the exotic, erotic East, they hurry back to their apartments to dream of sheep.

MY FRIEND BAAAARRY FROM N.Z.

This explains why New Zealand men only wear trousers with button-up flies; sheep have become alerted to the sound of zippers.

It also explains why most Kiwi men have names like Baaaarry or Baaaaaasil.

While the average expatriate man is perfectly able to father at least 520

GET BACK TO YOUR BED!!

DIRTY DAAAAAAANCING.

children during a 2-year stint in Singapore, the average New Zealander would have been able to father 13,498 sheep in the same period.

Most New Zealand expatriates arrive in Singapore during the lambing season, to avoid paternity suits.

BAAAAAABRA & BAAAABAAARRY

YANKS

Many Americans, coming from a very liberated society, perceive local girls as simply dumb blondes with black hair. When some American men realise that local girls have large, Western-sized breasts, they feel compelled to announce this fact to the girl in the certain belief that she might not have noticed.

After sleeping with an American, many local girls find it quite appropriate that the United States was the home of Custer's Last Stand.

Before being posted to Singapore, 91.3% of American expatriates thought it was an island off the coast of China. After living in Singapore, many American expatriates still think it is an island off the coast of China.

American expatriates are amazed to learn that they will not be mugged in Bedok (unless by another American).

Americans are also amazed that so many Singaporean girls have deep voices, hairy legs and Adam's apples.

Americans are a very polite people. American men, for example, never accept dates with local girls without first asking "How much?"

Americans are always determined to make a good impression on their host country. This is why they rarely associate with Australians.

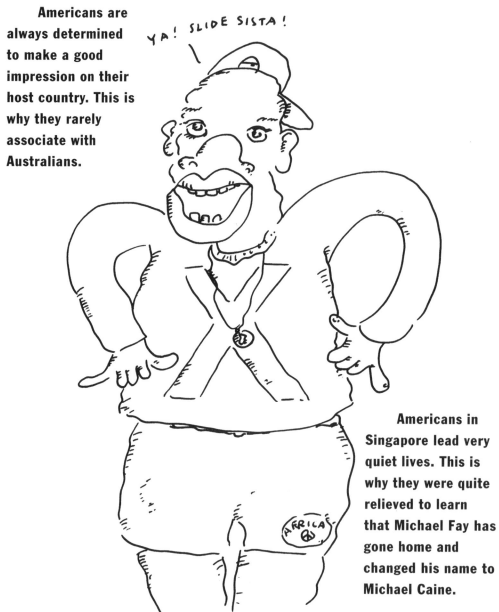

Americans in Singapore lead very quiet lives. This is why they were quite relieved to learn that Michael Fay has gone home and changed his name to Michael Caine.

FROGS

Frenchmen are supposed to be the world's best lovers. Well-dressed, passionate Frenchmen claim they can give a girl the most memorable night of her life. In reality, the night will be memorable for his rudeness and insatiable desire to talk about himself.

After a night with a Frenchman, a Singaporean girl fully understands why Mona Lisa has such a strange, bored smile.

THE SWISS

Because Switzerland is a neutral country, Swiss expatriates ensure their attempts at lovemaking are also neutral. Going to bed with a Swiss expatriate is about as exciting as spending Saturday afternoon in Geneva. (On second thoughts, it's probably better.) Most Swiss men expect their womenfolk to be called Heidi. The usual Heidi will have long, blonde hair. If she happens to have a large udder and a bell round her neck, also can. Many Swiss men believe they possess a male organ which would rival the Matterhorn, whereas local girls don't think their horns matter at all.

HIGH POWER SWISS BANKER

THE DUTCH

There is no truth in the rumour that Dutchmen prefer lesbians, despite the fact that Holland contains many dykes. Dutchmen are so oversexed that some of their cheeses are full of holes. In order to circulate with the opposite sex, many Dutchman make love to girls on windmills. As these aren't available in Singapore, he leads a celibate life.

Belgian men are always mistaken for Dutchmen, so they have even less luck.

The Dutch are the European masters of compromise. For example, if a Dutchman wants to buy a new car for Christmas, but his wife wants a fur coat instead, they will buy a fur coat and keep it in the garage.

Unfortunately, many Dutchmen find Singapore's cultural values somewhat disorienting. What is mandatory in Amsterdam is a hanging offence in Singapore.

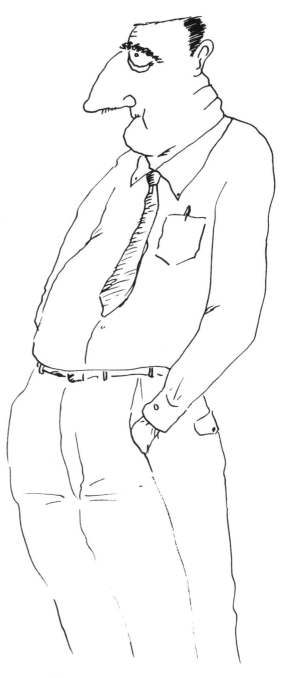

THE IRISH

A lot of people make very unfair jokes about the Irish. Actually, the Irish are very polite. For example, crowds of Irishmen can often be seen outside the brothels in Geylang. They are merely waiting for the red lights to turn green so they can go in.

THE POLES

The most disadvantaged group of expatriates are the Poles. No local girl can pronounce a name like Wczywszchywyszkski. If a Polish man fails to arouse a local girl with such scintillating conversational gems as "Zywsch wschyski wyzzywsch?" (which means "Hello, nice weather we're having, I suppose sex is out of the question?"), he will often pull a 9-inch sausage out

of his pocket to impress her. Sadly, many Polish men have been beaten to death with their own sausages.

The Poles are a very literal people. Polish expatriates are convinced that the Community Chest has something to do with the bust size of the average Singaporean woman. Some Poles even think that the Community Chest is a special nationwide breast-feeding facility.

Polish expatriates were shocked when they read 'The Official Guide to the Sarong Party Girl'. They were even more shocked when they learned that the Public Utilities Board (PUB) was going to change its name to Singapore Power and Gas (SPG). The thought of getting a bill every month from the SPG was bad enough; but having to go into the SPG Building to pay it was even more embarrassing.

Even worse: if you fell behind in your payments, you would have your water cut off by the SPG.

RUSSIANS

Russians, smelling of stale vodka and borsch, often try to pick up local girls without success. Usually they are surly sailors who have been shopping for cheap radios in High Street Centre. Local girls suspect them of KGB: Keeping Girls Bored.

SCANDINAVIANS

Should a Singaporean girl go to bed with a tall, blonde-headed man and ask "Are you finish, lah?", he will probably answer "No, I'm Swedish". The Scandinavians never go to brothels because they believe in free love. They are very proud of their Viking heritage; in fact, upon close inspection in the privacy of the bedroom, local girls can appreciate why Danish men are still called Erik the Red.

ITALIANS

The inventors of hair pollution, Italians are adding a dash of colour and noise to the expatriate community.

The Italians have taken over Boat Quay, where Singapore's best lasagne is offered as the first step in a romantic evening of passion.

According to rumour, Italians prefer to douse their girlfriends in garlic and olive oil, roll them in flour, and make love to them on a bed of pizza. This comes as a pleasant change after the Australians, who prefer to squirt beer over their girlfriends and roll them in a bed of old laundry.

ITALIAN MAFIA IN PINSTRIPE BOXER

CHAPTER 3

STYLO

ANG

MOHS

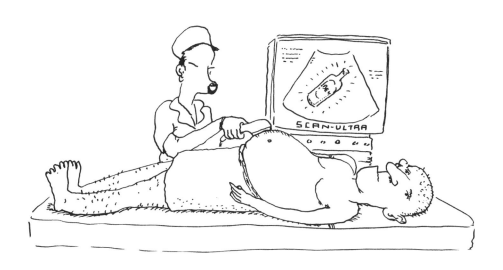

The average Singaporean girl has been portrayed as a sex-starved gold digger. While she might dream of escaping from her HDB estate, she has absolutely no intention of settling for one of the fat, aged members of the touring expatriate elite.

By wearing sunglasses to discos, and unbuttoning their shirts to their appendix scars, they firmly believe they can offer a local girl everything she needs: wit, charm, rugged good looks and a hugely expensive lifestyle.

However, many expatriates find that their disposable incomes are disposed of very quickly.

After paying the rent on their apartments in districts 9, 10 and 11, they manage to unload the rest of their money on booze, food and cars within one week. For the rest of the month, they sponge off their friends until the next payday.

As a result, very little money is available for clothes.

The preferred brand of expatriate underwear is Jockey, probably because jockeys are usually short. Most of the time their underwear remains invisible under an overhanging belly.

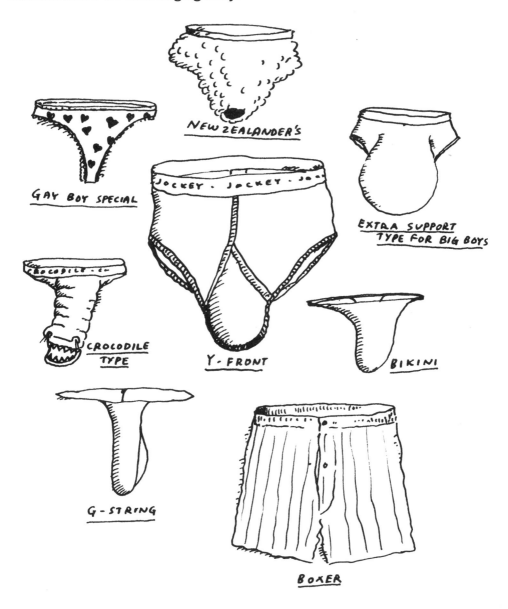

NEW ZEALANDER'S

GAY BOY SPECIAL

EXTRA SUPPORT TYPE FOR BIG BOYS

CROCODILE TYPE

Y - FRONT

BIKINI

G - STRING

BOXER

FIRST ATTEMPT AT WEARING A SARONG

Many expatriates wear sarongs, eat with their hands and even learn to use squat toilets. They believe this will make them more acceptable to locals. What they don't realise is that they become figures of fun because the last thing a local needs is a bluff local.

Other expatriates wear sarongs because their doctors have warned them to avoid wearing tight underpants in the tropics.

Sarongs keep British expatriates well ventilated, ensuring a free flow of fresh air to the parts which may not have been washed recently.

One Australian called John used to choose sarongs which matched his cheap floral ties.

Trouble was, after a night at Top Ten, he would arrive at the office the next morning wearing both the ties and the sarong.

Now he wears the ties under a discreet, strudel-coloured sarong to prevent any unseemly bulges in the batik.

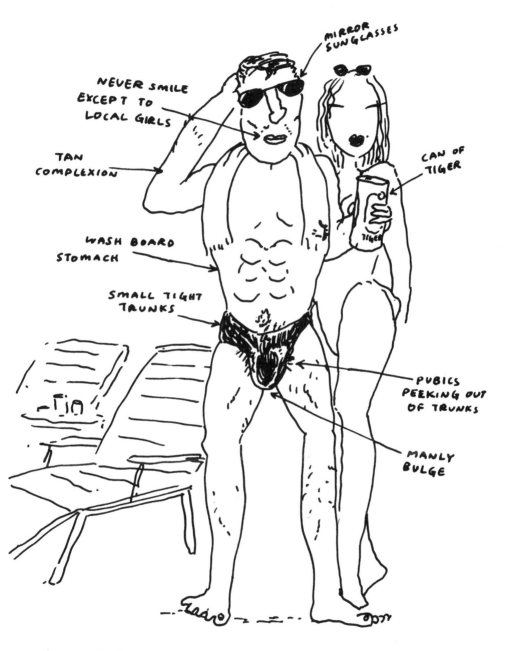

SOME EXPATS TRY TO LOOK BETTER THAN THEIR WOMAN

TYPICAL ANG MOH PANTS

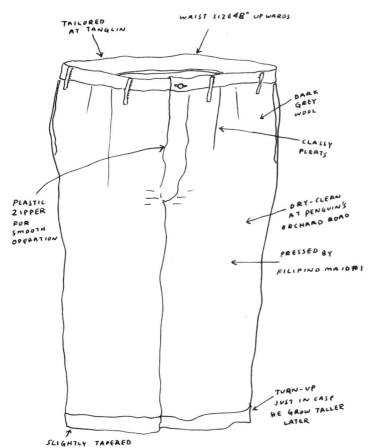

TAILORED AT TANGLIN

WAIST SIZE 48" UPWARDS

DARK GREY WOOL

CLASSY PLEATS

PLASTIC ZIPPER FOR SMOOTH OPERATION

DRY-CLEAN AT PENGUIN'S ORCHARD ROAD

PRESSED BY FILIPINO MAID #1

TURN-UP JUST IN CASE HE GROW TALLER LATER

SLIGHTLY TAPERED

Single expatriates are so named because they only have a single shirt, a single pair of Jockeys, a single pair of trousers and a single pair of socks.

15"

ANG MOH SHOE

73.9% of all expatriates have trouble finding shoes that fit them in Singapore. Expatriate feet usually demand at least size 11 or 12.

Sadly, 71.3% of all expatriates living in Towner Road have trouble finding their shoes in the first place. Either they fall off when riding

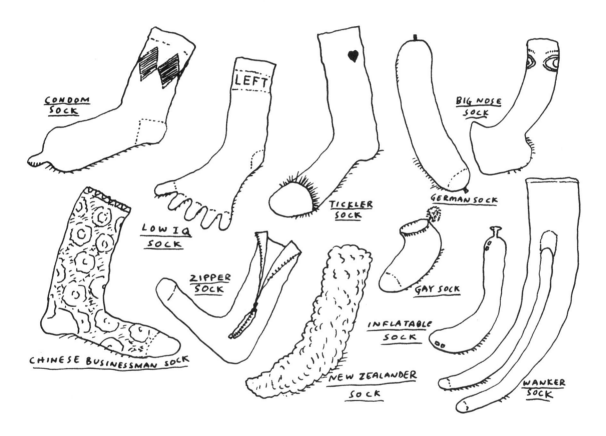

CONDOM SOCK

LEFT

BIG NOSE SOCK

TICKLER SOCK

GERMAN SOCK

LOW IQ SOCK

ZIPPER SOCK

CHINESE BUSINESSMAN SOCK

GAY SOCK

INFLATABLE SOCK

NEW ZEALANDER SOCK

WANKER SOCK

motorcycles naked at midnight, or they are thrown at strange women who demand money for services rendered.

85% of expatriates wear grey socks. Some expatriates, with names like Ashley or Antony, possess grey socks with little patterns stitched up the sides to indicate their colourful personalities.

Many expatriates suffer from halitosis. Their pungent breaths carry more than a whiff of garlic and alcohol. This explains why Asian girls prefer to kiss them virtually anywhere except on their mouths.

YOUR BREATH STINKS!

In order to convey the image of a rakish, youthful George Michaels, many middle-aged expatriates shave irregularly. An aggressive stubble, they think, will also lend a look of dangerous romance to an otherwise plain face. Unfortunately, most of their whiskers turn greyer than their socks.

DEAD RAZORS

25% MORE
INDUSTRIAL STRENGTH
MADE IN AUSTRALIA
D·O
FOR ALL KINDS OF B.O.
MASK OUT HARMFUL BODILY ODOURS!
SAY GOODBYE TO BEEF! MUTTON! BARBIE! SMELL!
CAUTION: MAKE YOU MORE ATTRACTIVE TO WOMEN OR MONEY BACK GUARANTEE

CAUTION: DO NOT USE IT ON PERSONAL ORGANS! USE DICK-O FOR THAT!
FOOTSIE
AUSSIE MADE FOOT POWER POWDER !!!
ELIMINATE SMELLY FOOT ODOUR! YOUR FEET NOW NO LONGER SMELL LIKE A DEAD RAT!
STOP SWEATS!

ANG MOH ESSENTIALS

IMPORTED TIRED OF BEING CALLED A WHITE CHICKEN? TRY POTENT AND DEADLY
PUBICS PLUS
ADD MORE HAIRS TO THE PART THAT REALLY MATTER MOST! NOW YOU CAN TELL YOUR LADY THAT YOU ARE A REAL MAN!
TESTED ON CHIMPANZEE!

DICK·O
SMELL FRESH DAILY KILL SMELLS THAT KNOCKS YOUR LADY OFF INSTANTLY! APPLY GENTLY ON SHAFT DAILY. INDUSTRIAL STRENGTH

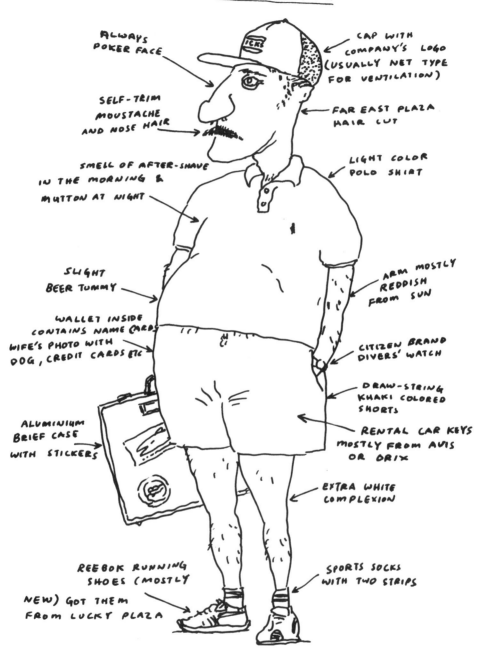

TYPICAL STYLISH ANGMOH

ALWAYS POKER FACE

CAP WITH COMPANY'S LOGO (USUALLY NET TYPE FOR VENTILATION)

SELF-TRIM MOUSTACHE AND NOSE HAIR

FAR EAST PLAZA HAIR CUT

SMELL OF AFTER-SHAVE IN THE MORNING & MUTTON AT NIGHT

LIGHT COLOR POLO SHIRT

SLIGHT BEER TUMMY

ARM MOSTLY REDDISH FROM SUN

WALLET INSIDE CONTAINS NAME CARDS WIFE'S PHOTO WITH DOG, CREDIT CARDS ETC

CITIZEN BRAND DIVERS' WATCH

DRAW-STRING KHAKI COLORED SHORTS

ALUMINIUM BRIEF CASE WITH STICKERS

RENTAL CAR KEYS MOSTLY FROM AVIS OR ORIX

EXTRA WHITE COMPLEXION

REEBOK RUNNING SHOES (MOSTLY NEW) GOT THEM FROM LUCKY PLAZA

SPORTS SOCKS WITH TWO STRIPS

Expatriate men say they prefer local girls with a mouth as big as a jacuzzi; you just hang your towel over the edge and jump in. The truth is, nothing is bigger than an expatriate mouth which is used exclusively to talk about its owner. Expatriate mouths have many other applications; for example, dentures can be trained to click in time to the music at discos.

Expatriates are supposed to drive big, important-looking cars or sexy sports cars. These days, however, the most an expatriate can aspire to is a Honda

Accord. By trashing his car after a party, he will end up driving a Honda Accordian.

For years, expatriates called local girls bicycles, because they represented free rides. Now, expatriates are often seen riding real bicycles to work.

They also called local girls taxis, because they were good for short trips. Now, expatriates rarely catch real taxis because taxi drivers won't offer credit.

Some expatriates are lucky enough to receive a car as part of their salary package. It is easy to recognise a car owned by a single expatriate: the springs in the back seat will have collapsed, and the door pockets will be full of old condoms.

Over 63% of all cars driven by single expatriates have at least five bottles of car freshener in use at the same time.

Lonely expatriates often crash their cars in order to inflate the airbags. The airbags make excellent substitutes for Asian women.

ANG MOH'S TOOTH BRUSH

The humble toothbrush is the expatriate's single most important possession. It can be used to remove scraps of week-old pizza from his shoes as well as his teeth. It also helps scrub dirt from his shirt collar, or any other place for that matter.

The toothbrush can be employed to remove unsightly rings from around his bathtub.

It helps remove baked-on grease from his microwave oven, thereby improving the flavour of his toothpaste the next morning.

Many Australians, who are great believers in hygienic sexual practices, offer their toothbrushes to their girlfriends to ensure they are spotlessly clean everywhere.

As a result of this generosity, one Australian called John lost, on average, five toothbrushes a week.

The British, of course, would never share their toothbrushes with anyone in case the toothbrush was lost and they were deprived of ten minutes in front of a mirror.

No one in living memory has ever asked a Pole if they could borrow his toothbrush.

New Zealanders have invented a toothbrush with woollen bristles, as this reminds them of happier times at home.

Expatriates love going on holidays to exotic places like Phuket, Pattaya and Perth.

Eastern mysticism is an irresistible lure, such as sleeping with local women and exploring cultural sites like discos and brothels.

Single expatriates are keen to discover Asian values. In certain cities, these values are as little as US$100 a night.

Some expatriates prefer to travel by yacht to isolated beaches in Thailand. They frequently invite local girls to join them on these cruises, better known as Boat Rides to Hell.

Australians are especially favoured as crew members because they can be counted on to drop their shorts faster than they can drop anchor.

AIRPLANE FULL OF ANG MOHS
APPROACH TOUCH DOWN

The Australians drink tinnies of beer from the minute the yacht sails to the minute it sinks. Their favourite sport is trying to find out what their female companions will lose first: their consciousness or their bikinis.

Australian yachtsmen are a big hit in Thai restaurants. They perform such Aussie feats as The Tom Yam Chunder and the Pineapple Rice Ruuuuuuth. Should one of these yachts ever meet a boatload of Vietnamese refugees, the boat people will be invited on board to celebrate their liberation. After which, the Vietnamese will immediately turn back for Ho Chi Minh City.

Amazingly, these yachts are never intercepted by pirates. No self-respecting pirate would want to get involved.

Country by country, culture by culture, expatriates on holiday are determined to leave their mark.

In Taipei's karaoke lounges, Taiwanese businessmen can now remove their clothes, stand on the table and sing "Waltzing Matilda".

On Tokyo's Ginza, flocks of New Zealand businessmen have trained their

THAI WAITRESS

Japanese counterparts to treat women like sheep. (Any girl in Tokyo wearing a lambswool sweater is definitely not safe.)

Even in Hong Kong, thousands of visiting Americans have taught their business associates to be loud in restaurants.

Expatriates always have difficulty remembering Asian names. For this reason, girls in Manila and Bangkok now wear numbers. And, in some cases, so do the men.

Oddly enough, Asian hotel owners actually prefer to have expatriates as guests. While other tourists are determined to remove the hotel's taps, telephones and towels, the average expatriate tourist is perfectly content to remove the local sarongs, saris and cheongsams.

When expatriates travel on holiday around Asia, they carry the following essential equipment:

OF COURSE, OUR SERVICE IS IMPECCABLE.

1. Twelve packets of standard condoms, preferably new,
2. Six packets of electronically reinforced condoms, also preferably new,
3. One change of underwear and a packet of Lomotil,
4. One sarong so they can blend in with the locals,
5. One gaudy Hawaiian shirt so they can stand out from the locals,
6. One pair of walking socks, which can also double up as a condom in an emergency,
7. One packet of Panadol in case they meet a girl with a headache,
8. A mirror, so they won't get lonely,
9. A disposable razor so they can shave under their arms to ward off tropical rashes,
10. A copy of the SPG book so they can maintain a feeling of superiority,
11. A packet of luminous condoms so they can locate it in the dark.

STD *In Asia, this stands for Sexually Transmitted Disease. In Australia, it stands for Sexually Transmitted Drudgery.*

CHAPTER 4

ANG MOHS

AT

WORK

Is it true that Caucasians working in Singapore would not be able to get jobs in their own countries, or anywhere else in the world?

Of course not. To prove this point, here are just some of the jobs currently available in other countries:

AUSTRALIA

158 garbage collectors in Melbourne

85 garbage collectors in Brisbane

76 used car salesmen in Perth

25 Vice Squad detectives in Sydney

1 Prime Minister

BRITAIN

5,000 taxi drivers

3,000 bus drivers

1 Ambassador to Malaysia

1 Governor for Hong Kong

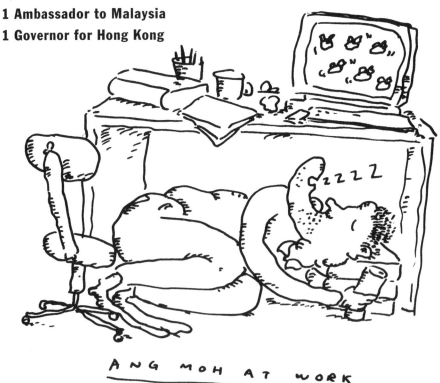

ANG MOH AT WORK

NEW ZEALAND
350 sheep farmers
225 assistant sheep farmers
1 veterinary surgeon (obstetrics)
SWITZERLAND
3,000 comedians

In Hong Kong, expatriates were once called FILTH (Failed In London, Try Hongkong). In Singapore they are more likely to be called PIGS (Perth Impossible, Go Singapore).

OIL RIGGERS

Oil riggers sleep with their cowboy boots on. Their huge beer bellies mean that it can take up to half an hour for them to locate their drilling bits. (Sometimes they fall asleep before they can.) Oilies like to play Willie Nelson music and wear Harley Davidson singlets. Their lurid tattoos have been designed to attract the attention of local girls. The most popular designs are:

1. Naked women,
2. Naked serpents,
3. Naked women and naked serpents,
4. Their mothers.

Oilies, however, are a very unpretentious lot, and what you see is what you get.

TYPICAL MACHO TATTOO

Unlike advertising men. They always present themselves very well, packaged in crisp white shirts and floral ties. However, they seem to have forgotten that good advertising is the fastest way to kill a bad product.

ADVERTISING

Most expatriates in advertising consider themselves superior in both intellect and sexual capability. With a couple of notable exceptions, this is not true. Most advertising expatriates base their orgasms on television commercials and come in either 10 or 30 seconds. Expatriate art directors believe that foreplay consists of telling a local girl how many awards they have won.

Expatriate advertising executives visit Newton Circus twice a night. Once, at 8pm, to have dinner. And again, at 3.30am, in a last, desperate search for a free local girl to sleep with.

Marketing executives spend more time marketing themselves to local women than marketing their products.

HOTEL INDUSTRY

The hotel industry employs a range of expatriates which caters to no girl's taste. Many local girls are convinced that the shape of a chef's hat serves only to indicate what is uppermost on his mind. In reality, a pastry chef's cakes rise faster than he can.

Hotel managers are a very fussy lot. On the rare occasions when they succeed in getting a local girl into bed, they run their fingers over her body to check for dust.

Executives in hotel marketing departments are usually English, Welsh or Australian. They see women in the same terms as they do their hotels: Occupancy Levels. Any girl they haven't occupied is an immediate challenge. They also keep secret diaries and rate their girl friends from one-star to five-star. The only trouble is, they never ask the girls to rate them.

LE CHEF

THE MUSIC INDUSTRY

Expatriates from the music capitals of the world — Vienna, Budapest, Paris, Perth, Bondi and Auckland — have flooded into Singapore. Refined Europeans concentrate on strings, leaving the horns to the Australians.

Ang moh recording engineers do more mixing at Brannigans than they

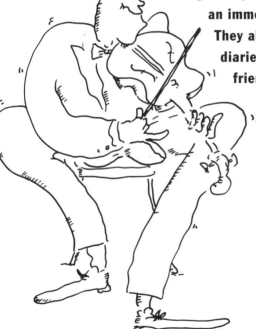

ANG MOHS ARE MORE EXPRESSIVE. IS THAT WHY THE SSO IS FULL OF THEM?

do in their studios.

Kiwi musicians can be spotted carrying their bassoons and piccolos in little knitted covers.

AIRLINES

Expatriate pilots and flight engineers have been attracted to Singapore by the promise of better terms and conditions. The girls are in better condition and the terms are cheaper.

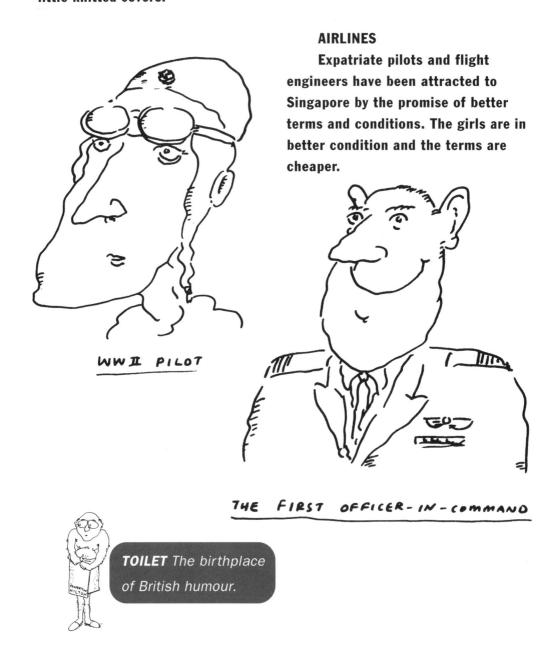

WW II PILOT

THE FIRST OFFICER-IN-COMMAND

TOILET The birthplace of British humour.

BANKING

Australian banking executives have a deep and abiding interest in the bottom line. Aussie bankers (which appropriately rhymes with Aussie wankers) have many endearing habits. Some write their names and telephone numbers on their underpants, in the hope that when a local girl finds them in her bed she will invite them back for a second round.

British bankers, on the other hand, display much greater dignity and tact. They staple their business cards to a local girl's panties and mail them back to her with her statement.

Whereas Swiss bankers, obsessed with secrecy, would simply keep her panties and never reveal their own names at all.

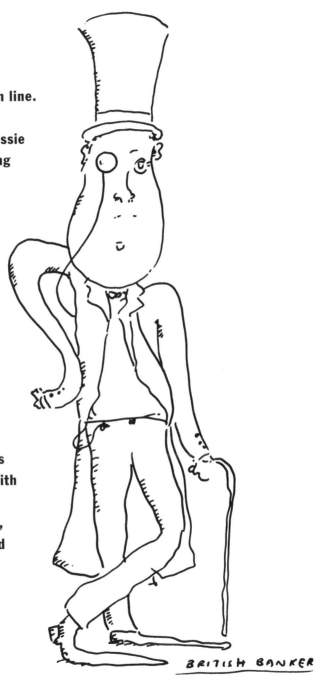

BRITISH BANKER

THE SECRET OF SUCCESS —
TEAMWORK!

Traditionally, expatriates have been hired because they can do things which Singaporeans can't. Like it or not, this is still true:

1. No Singaporean can break wind noisily in a board meeting and then laugh about it,
2. No Singaporean can ride a motor cycle stark naked past the Tanglin Police Station,
3. No Singaporean can go drinking every night at Brannigans and breathe alcoholic fumes over his secretary the next morning,

ARE YOU THE CREAM OF THE CROP?
EXPAT BOSS LOOKING FOR SECRETARY
- PLEASANT PERSONALITY
- WILLING TO LEARN
- OUT GOING INDIVIDUAL
- SINGLE, WILLING TO TRAVEL FREQUENTLY
- ATTRACTIVE SALARY PACKAGE

CALL OR WRITE TO:
THE PERSONNEL MGR
P.O. BOX 76529
SINGAPORE 366
TEL: 8707080
ATTACHED RECENT PHOTO WILL BE AN ADVANTAGE

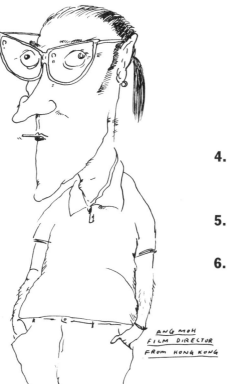

ANG MOH FILM DIRECTOR FROM HONG KONG

4. No Singaporean can be rude and tactless to his most important clients,
5. No Singaporean can go to work without his underpants,
6. No Singaporean can go to work with his underpants over his trousers.

A CHINESE LAWYER

A NEW ZEALAND LAWYER

Naturally, the average expatriate puts a lot into his job. A lot of wasted time, a lot of drinking, a lot of superiority.

Visiting white executives will prefer to deal with him rather than the local Asian executives.

This is because he knows all the best restaurants, all the best girlie bars, and has exclusive use of the company charge card.

The fact that he is a male nymphomaniac is entirely irrelevant.

He will always load the company with bad debts, but then nobody has ever heard of good debts, so why should he worry?

CHAPTER 5

ANG

MOH

FOOD

ANG MOH HAVING A TASTE
OF HIS OWN MEDICINE

Judging by the size of the average ang moh, he enjoys his food even more than the average Singaporean. But what kind of food?

AUSTRALIAN CUISINE
That's like a heading which says Australian Culture. Let's start again:

AUSTRALIAN FOOD
Australians believe that what you eat today, walks and talks tomorrow. So their relentless diet of meat pies, sausage rolls and battered savs has a lot to answer for. If it's not covered in pastry, it's covered in batter.

Australians also swear by (but never at) a peculiar substance called Vegemite. It is actually a yeast extract, which means it is made by scraping out dozens of beer barrels into a little glass jar. Vegemite is designed to be spread over anything and everything: bread, biscuits, kids' faces and even women. This remarkable black paste is renowned for being able to put hair on your chest. (Ask any Australian woman, she'll tell you.)

VEGEMITE SANDWICH

Australians also have a passion for a biscuit called the Iced Vo-Vo, famous for its jam topping sprinkled with coconut. If the Chinese burn a Mercedes-Benz so they can have one in Heaven, then the Aussies would burn Iced Vo-Vo's. (Vegemite, of course, does not burn.) Australians would probably go to war to defend the Iced Vo-Vo biscuit factory, the only one of its kind in the world. Even an Australian called John would happily trade his collection of cheap floral ties for one packet of Iced Vo-Vo's.

Another uniquely Australian invention is the Jaffa. This ball of chocolate coated in orange candy is suitable for rolling away down the aisles of

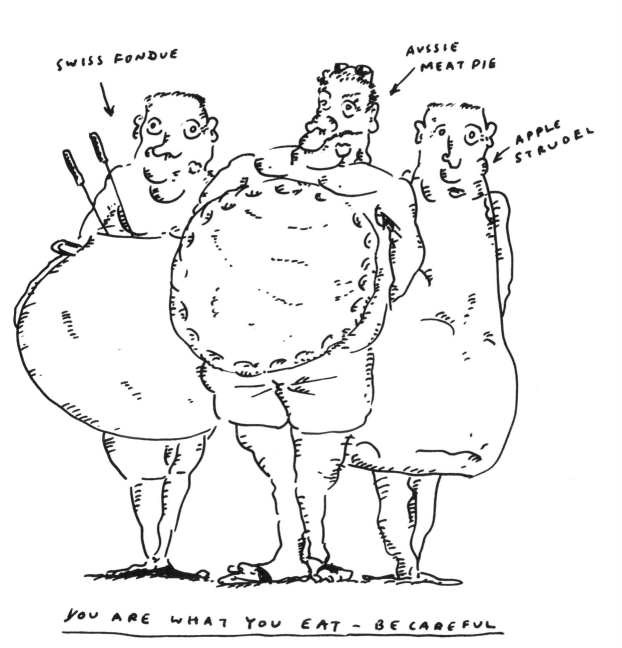

YOU ARE WHAT YOU EAT — BE CAREFUL

FROZEN USA CHICKEN

CHICKEN ARSE

OF COURSE EVERY PART

CHICKEN CLAWS

CHINESE BELIEVE EVERY PART
OF A CHICKEN IS EDIBLE

cinemas during the most dramatic moments of "Schindler's List" or "Lassie Come Home". Because Jaffas rattle in their packets, Australian perverts never keep them in their trouser pockets.

AMERICAN FOOD

American cuisine is best known for Deep Fried Chicken, which originated in the Deep South where certain members of society were themselves deep fried from time to time.

The Americans also invented Clam Chowder (Hairy Clam Chowder also can) and the Turkey. Turkey is consumed on Thanksgiving Day, so named because they give thanks they only have to eat it once a year.

The Turkey is such a revered bird in America that even Presidents are named after it.

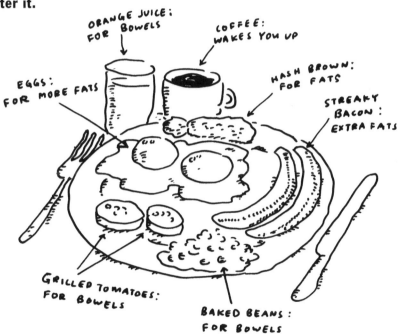

AMERICAN STYLE BREAKFAST
BASIC TYPE

BRITISH FOOD

The British diet consists of pork pies, fish and chips, roast lamb and roast beef. No surprises here; just good solid stuff for stuffing good solid people.

However, the British are an ingenious lot and centuries ago discovered how to recycle their leftovers. One such dish is called Bubble & Squeak, a mixture of potato and cabbage fried up for a quick breakfast. Appropriately enough, the Brits also invented the Upside Down Cake and the Tart.

British sausages are one of the world's greatest mysteries. Nobody quite knows what goes into them, least of all the people who make them.

The Bread and Butter Pudding is a cunning way to turn stale bread and dubious butter into a dessert. After eating this concoction, an Englishman will immediately skip sex and fall fast asleep. (The alternative, of course, would be to make love to the woman who made it.)

The British are amongst the world's greatest consumers of baked beans, which probably explains why the British Lion could roar so loudly.

During the Second World War, thousands of British troops ate baked beans. The thunderous noise which followed led Rommel to believe he was totally outnumbered.

In order to save money and conserve ammunition, all 21-gun salutes fired nowadays in Britain are actually performed by 21 soldiers who have eaten 21 cans of baked beans. This also explains the strange, slightly pained expressions on the faces of the Royal Family in recent months.

In Singapore, the penalty for discharging a can of baked beans in any public place carries a fine of $1,000.

Any local girl is advised to thoroughly check a British expatriate's rubbish bin for empty baked bean cans before spending a night with him.

NEW ZEALAND FOOD

New Zealanders are cannibals, eating lamb chops and roast lamb.

Sheep's brains are even fed to innocent children, to ensure each generation is able to relate to its nearest relatives.

CONTINENTAL CUISINE

Adventurous and quirky cuisine begins in France. The French loathe baked beans as Paris is noisy enough. Instead, they clamour for such delicacies as snails and amputated frogs.

The Italians will have none of the above. They prefer food which has been saturated in oil, garlic and onions. As far as Italians are concerned, the word polyunsaturated refers to a dry parrot.

The Swiss, on the other hand, are addicted to cheese. The Swiss fondue requires grown men and women to stab stale chunks of bread into a pot of bubbling cheese. After eating a heavy fondue, it is no wonder the Swiss have never been attacked by another European country.

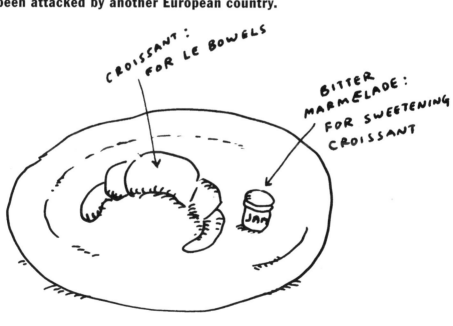

CROISSANT: FOR LE BOWELS

BITTER MARMELADE: FOR SWEETENING CROISSANT

JAM

CONTINENTAL BREAKFAST

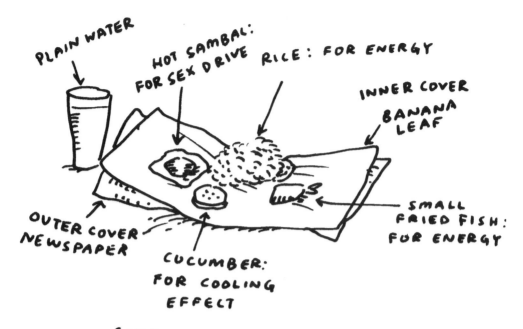

PLAIN WATER

HOT SAMBAL: FOR SEX DRIVE

RICE: FOR ENERGY

INNER COVER BANANA LEAF

OUTER COVER NEWSPAPER

CUCUMBER: FOR COOLING EFFECT

SMALL FRIED FISH: FOR ENERGY

SINGAPOREAN BREAKFAST

When expatriates arrive in Singapore, many are shocked to find an entirely different cuisine to that in their own home countries.

The British, for instance, still cannot believe that anyone would want to eat anything other than sensible British food.

The sportier European types will immediately gravitate to exotically spicy local food. Being highly inventive, the Swiss have found a way to add cheese to curries. The Australians, of course, will eat anything, providing they can first drown it with beer. Australian gourmets are easily recognised: they're the ones who go to classy restaurants and order the Day of the Soup.

The British actually bring their own toilet paper to local restaurants.

In European culture, no meal is complete without wine.

Once the rule was "red meat, red wine" and vice-versa. These days, the gourmet is free to drink any wine he chooses. At an intimate dinner party

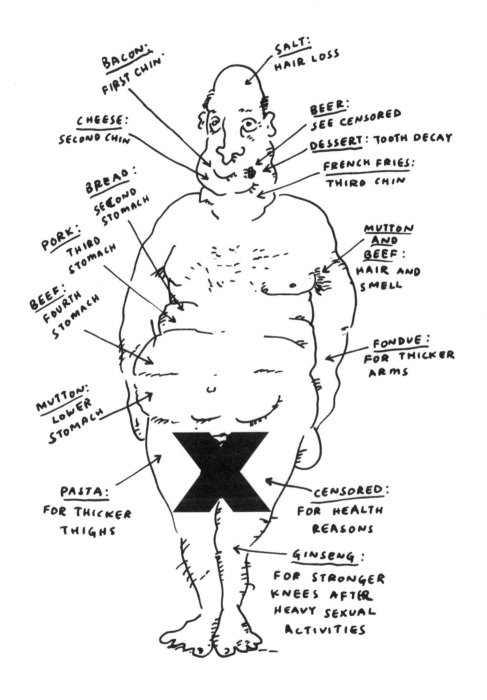

FOOD: WHERE IT ALL GOES

with an Australian, most of the wine will end up on the girl anyhow. Or worse, the floor.

In the old days, grapes were actually crushed by foot. As wine consumption grew, productivity had to increase; this explains why European feet are so big.

It also explains why Europeans have very small gaps between their toes, so that no grape can escape.

A lot of snobbery still surrounds wine. Even if the wine is not made in France, it will have a French name. This is to convince you it must be good wine and worth the high price it is selling for. American wines, however, are quite cheap. For this reason, they are often displayed next to the detergents and floor cleaners.

A lot of fuss is made about Scotch whisky, too. Only the ang mohs could worship something which starts life in a Scottish bog. Fortunately, whisky does not have to be crushed, thereby saving the Scots the bother of washing their kilts. Because whisky is so expensive, a lot of people accuse the Scots of being mean. In truth, the meanest people in the world can be found in Singapore bookshops, standing around and reading books without paying for them.

Gin is a great favourite of the English. It used to be called "mother's ruin". Quite right, too. When the English started growing rubber in Malaysia, they started drinking a lot of gin. After a few gins, they actually thought they owned the place. After a few more, they actually thought they owned India, too.

Singapore has the cleanest bar floors of any country in the world. This is because the only alcoholic beverage ever invented in Singapore is XO Beer, which is meant to be taken lying down. Because so many horizontal New Zealanders are now drinking XO Beer, the next product on the market will be XO Sweaters.

CHAPTER 6

HOW THE SINGAPORE MAN SHAPES UP

CHINESE MAN ENTERING CBD ZONE

Why do so many Singaporean girls complain about local men?

Well, unlike expatriate men, local men generally have hairless bodies. This enables a girl to check the merchandise more carefully.

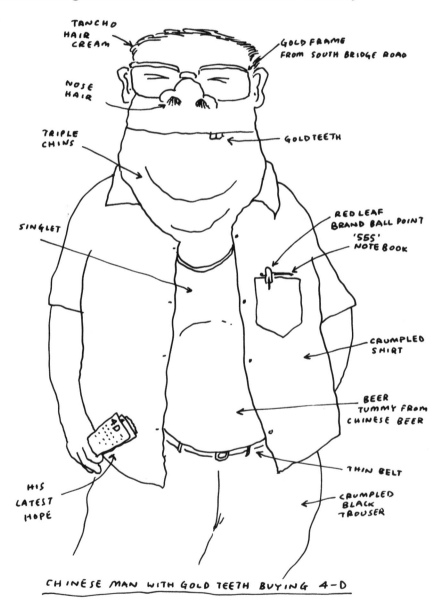

CHINESE MAN WITH GOLD TEETH BUYING 4-D

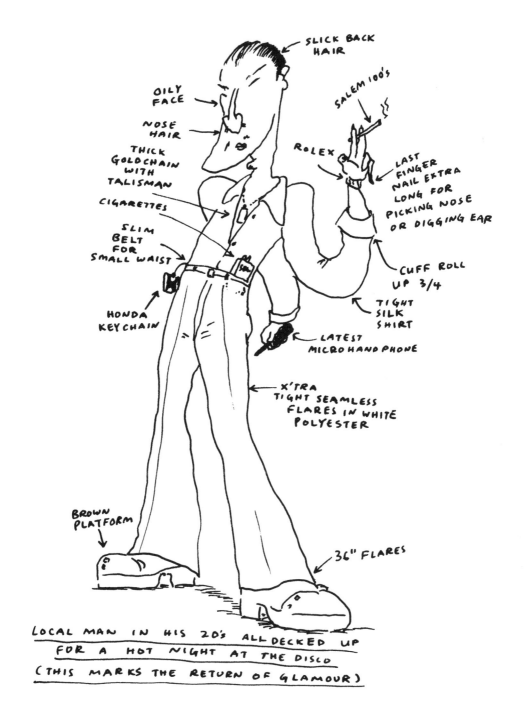

SLICK BACK
HAIR

OILY
FACE

NOSE
HAIR

THICK
GOLD CHAIN
WITH
TALISMAN

CIGARETTES

SLIM
BELT
FOR
SMALL WAIST

HONDA
KEY CHAIN

SALEM 100's

ROLEX

LAST
FINGER
NAIL EXTRA
LONG FOR
PICKING NOSE
OR DIGGING EAR

CUFF ROLL
UP 3/4

TIGHT
SILK
SHIRT

LATEST
MICRO HAND PHONE

X'TRA
TIGHT SEAMLESS
FLARES IN WHITE
POLYESTER

BROWN
PLATFORM

36" FLARES

LOCAL MAN IN HIS 20's ALL DECKED UP
FOR A HOT NIGHT AT THE DISCO
(THIS MARKS THE RETURN OF GLAMOUR)

According to some, the average Singapore man's physique is too bony, all elbows and knees, and his extruded plastic flip-flops are about as romantic as the way he picks his teeth at Jack's Place.

Others say his greatest physical achievement is being able to stand on one leg in a hawker centre waiting for his fish balls.

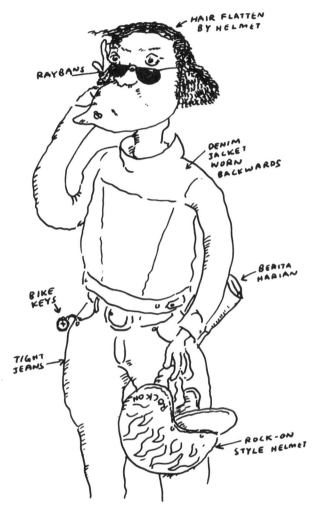

DESPATCH GUY

- HAIR FLATTEN BY HELMET
- RAYBANS
- DENIM JACKET WORN BACKWARDS
- BERITA HARIAN
- BIKE KEYS
- TIGHT JEANS
- ROCK-ON STYLE HELMET

Many refuse to marry a man whose whole life centres around the 3 M's: his Mother, his Mistress and his Mont Blanc.

58% of all local men are obsessed by business and careers. Another 40% are very laid back, and like their women to be laid back, too. The remaining 2% are still having their hair permed.

37% of all Singaporean women have their first experiences with local men at student parties, where the opposite sexes remain less opposite. These parties, at homes located in the better suburbs, take place while the parents are away and raise more than just eyebrows.

ZOUKETTE

51% of Singaporean women are swept off their feet by dinner (usually at a satay stall). A further 33% have been whisked off to the beach at midnight (preferably the one at Lamp Post 150 opposite the Changi Airport Hangar).

Many local men promise their womenfolk an impressive car. Others promise the thrill of a motorbike ride, with her legs pointing out into the traffic and her fifty cent coins displayed to the world.

While expatriate men pride themselves on their sexual experience, many local men grow up in blissful ignorance of the female body. (In some cases, the last time they saw a woman's breast was when they were being weaned.)

According to Singaporean girls, 65% of local men cannot cook their own

CHINESE LOVERS *It is the dream of every Ah Beng to go to bed and be called Ahhhhhhhhhhhhhhhhh, Beng.*

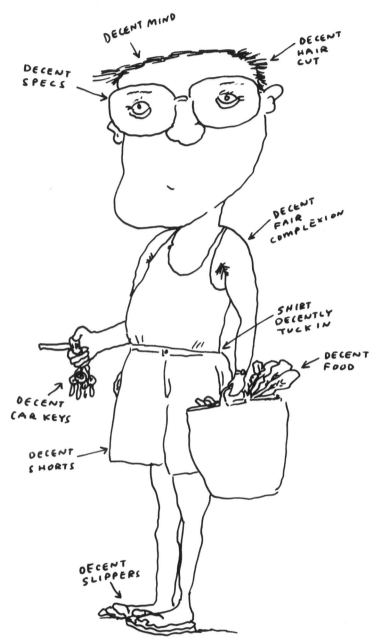

DECENT MIND

DECENT HAIR CUT

DECENT SPECS

DECENT FAIR COMPLEXION

SHIRT DECENTLY TUCK IN

DECENT FOOD

DECENT CAR KEYS

DECENT SHORTS

DECENT SLIPPERS

A DECENT FAMILY MAN USUALLY DO ALL THE MARKETING

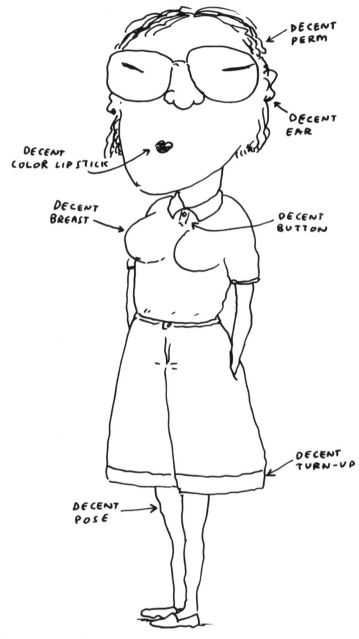

DECENT
PERM

DECENT
EAR

DECENT
COLOR LIPSTICK

DECENT
BREAST

DECENT
BUTTON

DECENT
TURN-UP

DECENT
POSE

DECENT HOUSEWIFE WAITING FOR KIDS AT YAMAHA MUSIC SCHOOL

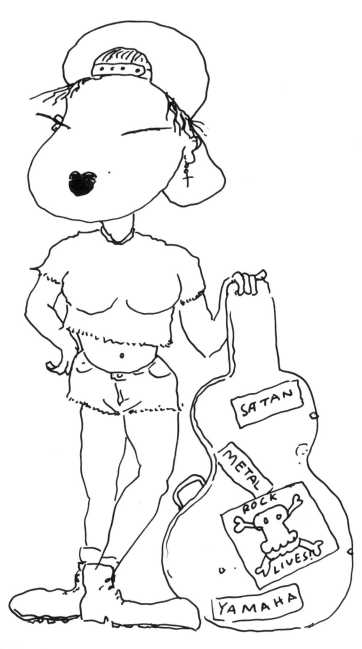

NOT SO DECENT DAUGHTER

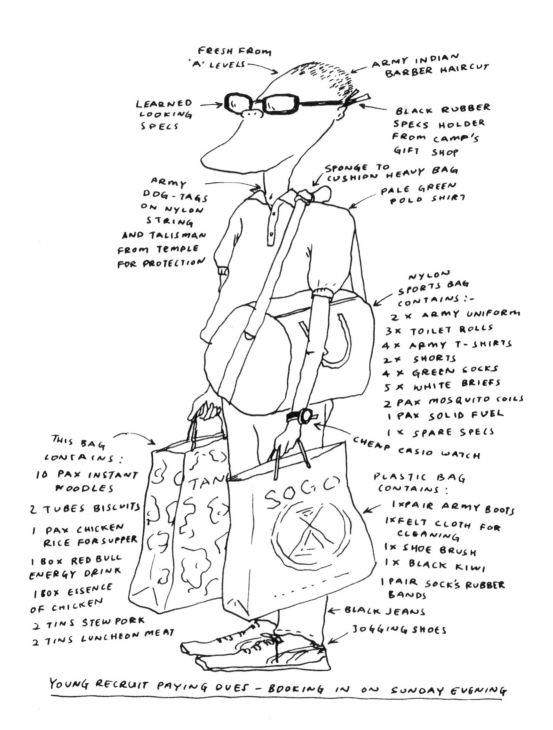

YOUNG RECRUIT PAYING DUES - BOOKING IN ON SUNDAY EVENING

meals; 49% cannot iron a shirt; 32% cannot make a bowl of Maggi Mee; 28% cannot make a cup of tea; and 13% just cannot.

While Caucasian men frequent discos to pick up women, local men are far more subtle. They go to expensive KTV lounges and fondle the hostesses. When the bill arrives they stop singing and start screaming.

If they are lucky enough, the mamasan will arrange for them to take one of the hostesses out for the night. He has to be careful, of course: it's not that the hostess will have AIDS, but she could well be a typist from his own company, or even his daughter.

Local men see nothing wrong with this behaviour. Their philosophy is: 'If you put cake in front of me, sure to eat'.

Some local men, if they are rich enough, will take a second wife. Surprisingly, a lot of women are perfectly happy to become minor wives. At least she won't have to put up with him on a full-time basis.

Many local girls find they have more freedom dealing

MOLESTER
TYPE 2(A)
POLICE
CATEGORY

with a Caucasian man than a local man. A local man always comes with family ties. You marry him, you marry his mother. You also marry his grandmother, what to do?

Some local men are very mother-tied and too opinionated (his mother's opinions, not his). Before he can go out on Saturday night he has to:

1.   Clean his room,
2.   Do the shopping,
3.   Babysit his brother,
4.   Clean his father's Nissan pickup truck,
5.   Clean his handphone,

6. Polish his shoes until they are shiny enough for him to see his mother's reflection,
7. Eat porridge to keep up his strength,
8. Dub Cantonese tapes for his mother,
9. Clean up his room again after eating porridge.

Many local men also prefer to marry girls who are less intelligent than they are, which narrows the field considerably.

MAN IN BUS, SHOWING OFF HIS MANHOOD

Of course, local men pride themselves on their frugality, which turns off many local girls. She can't understand a man who walks six blocks into the CBD to save $3, and then splurges $500 on a bottle of XO for his mates in the KTV lounge.

The worst type of local men are of course the *boh-sia* boys, better known as Sarong Party Boys.

Usually they work in hotels and latch on to lonely Japanese and Caucasian women.

Japanese girls visiting Singapore are away from their cloistered lives in Kyoto. They feel totally uninhibited, and the SPB will ensure she does not remain totally uninhibited.

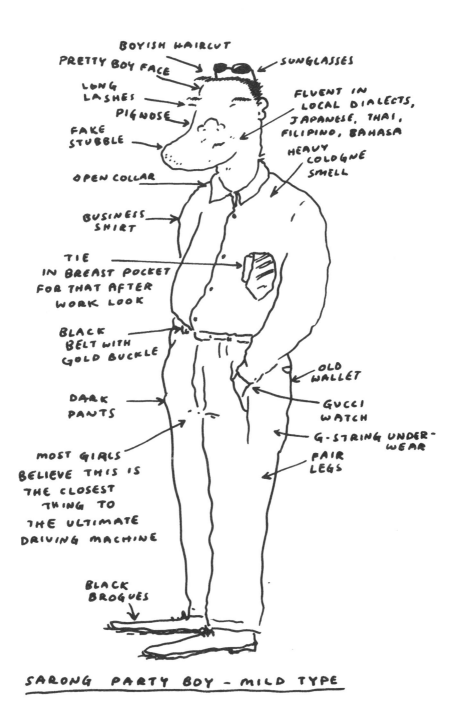

BOYISH HAIRCUT

PRETTY BOY FACE

SUNGLASSES

LONG LASHES

FLUENT IN LOCAL DIALECTS, JAPANESE, THAI, FILIPINO, BAHASA

PIGNOSE

FAKE STUBBLE

HEAVY COLOGNE SMELL

OPEN COLLAR

BUSINESS SHIRT

TIE IN BREAST POCKET FOR THAT AFTER WORK LOOK

BLACK BELT WITH GOLD BUCKLE

OLD WALLET

GUCCI WATCH

DARK PANTS

G-STRING UNDER-WEAR

FAIR LEGS

MOST GIRLS BELIEVE THIS IS THE CLOSEST THING TO THE ULTIMATE DRIVING MACHINE

BLACK BROGUES

SARONG PARTY BOY - MILD TYPE

The SPB will take her on a reckless whirl through the Orchard Road shops where she will shower him with little gifts. In return, he will spend a couple of nights in her room, jumping up at odd intervals to answer his pager.

Japanese girls have very short legs, so it is quite easy to catch them. Also, like all Japanese tourists, they will be trained to follow anything the SPB chooses to hold up high.

For the Japanese girl, a few nights in Singapore will be the equivalent of a few nights in Bangkok for the Japanese businessman. Japanese girls are very passionate in bed, and once roused she will soon exhaust the SPB. In fact, 78.5% of all Japanese women require at least 5.7 SPBs to satisfy their needs on an average visit.

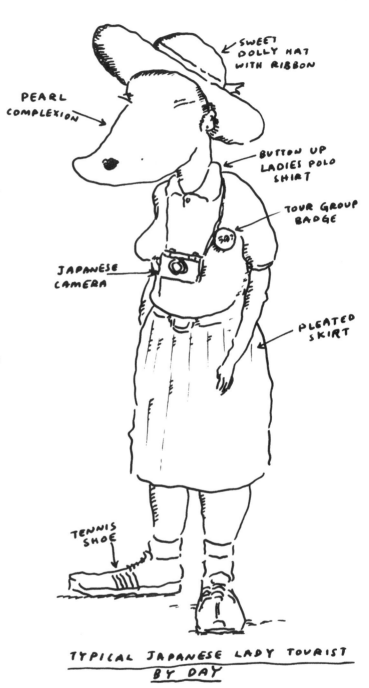

SWEET DOLLY HAT WITH RIBBON

PEARL COMPLEXION

BUTTON UP LADIES POLO SHIRT

TOUR GROUP BADGE

JAPANESE CAMERA

PLEATED SKIRT

TENNIS SHOE

TYPICAL JAPANESE LADY TOURIST BY DAY

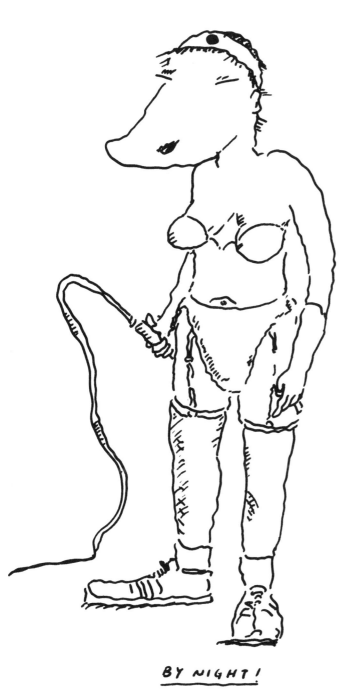

BY NIGHT!

81.3% of all Japanese women visiting Singapore will increase the girth of their thigh muscles by 10.3% during their stay.

Japanese women will teach the SPB a whole new range of sexual techniques, including the kamikaze bed dive.

Caucasian women are also very keen to explore the world of the Sarong Party Boy. They find SPBs an interesting diversion from their big, hulking husbands at home. A slim Chinese lad with a handphone and white socks represents a completely alien sexual challenge.

Heavyset Aussie women can usually consume 8.4 SPBs in a week. They will teach the SPB how to make love while barbecuing sausages. Due to her hairy legs, many SPBs become totally disoriented and suffer from homosexual guilt pangs.

Continental women are

more subtle. A Swedish girl with long, blonde hair and an hour-glass figure can actually crush an SPB during intercourse.

SPBs prefer gentler English women who are accustomed to less aggressive menfolk. With luck, he can accept her gifts and money and then fall asleep, just like a typical Englishmen. If she falls asleep first, he can while away the hours using his calculator to count her freckles.

Then there are the other kind of SPBs: the Sarong Party Bapuk, or transvestites, who hate SPGs but try to imitate them. The average bapuk spends three hours getting dressed, but when he has picked up a rich foreign businessman he can be stripped and ready for action in three seconds.

Geylang is the preferred location for a quiet interlude with a Sarong Party Bapuk. Because the bapuk spends all his money on clothes, he will usually live with other bapuk.

So a lonely foreigner will find himself sharing the same mattress with:

6 drama queens,

2 pet cats,

3 other lonely foreigners,

2 relatives from Malaysia,

STORY GOES LIKE THIS: MAN INVITED A TRANSVESTITE TO HIS ROOM AND WAS GAGGED AND ROBBED

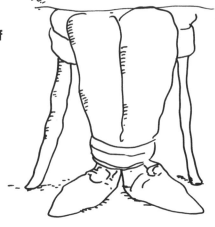

AT THE HAIRDRESSER

the landlord collecting his dues,
2 hairdressers,
1 cooking pot,
2 bottles of water,
5 ashtrays (full),
And last week's laundry.

Like every society in the world, Singapore produces its crop of Local Gigolos. With names like Robert, Michael, Andy, Alan or K.C., they haunt swimming clubs, tennis courts and even upscale country clubs.

They target rich, bored housewives seeking a discreet midweek afternoon of fun and frolic in his nicely furnished apartment. Only when the Gigolo has lured the housewife into his bedroom will he dare to remove his shirt.

He is probably a real estate salesman, which explains why he is able to roam free during the day. It also explains why he is happy to accept any commissions from the women who have enjoyed his company.

He is a very sporting chap, able to switch from golf to tennis at a moment's notice, depending on which club offers the best prospects. His greatest assets include his handphone,

LOCAL GIGOLO AT THE SWIMMING CLUB

EUNUCH

106

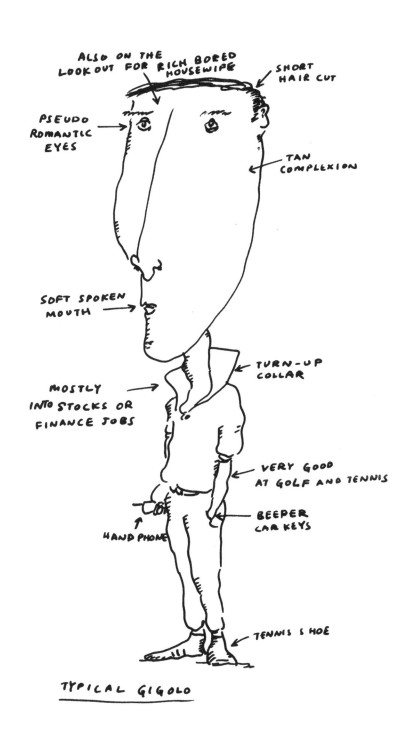

ALSO ON THE
LOOK OUT FOR RICH BORED HOUSEWIFE

SHORT
HAIR CUT

PSEUDO
ROMANTIC
EYES

TAN
COMPLEXION

SOFT SPOKEN
MOUTH

TURN-UP
COLLAR

MOSTLY
INTO STOCKS OR
FINANCE JOBS

VERY GOOD
AT GOLF AND TENNIS

BEEPER
CAR KEYS

HAND PHONE

TENNIS SHOE

TYPICAL GIGOLO

his year-round sun tan, and his priceless collection of sports shirts. Active only during the day, he retreats to his tanning machine at night.

The Gigolo is a distant relative of another phenomenon: the SPV, or Sarong Pervert.

SPVs gather at public swimming pools to catch odd glimpses of female flesh. They also wander along the East Coast Parkway, their eyes probing the doorways of public toilets and changing rooms. SPVs are actually terrified of women. In fact, the only women that 93.7% of SPVs have ever spoken to are their mothers.

SPVs occasionally enter the water, usually at the shallow end where they can remove their bathing costumes while balancing on one leg. SPVs are generally recognised by their rat-like noses and pinched faces, and their love of large, grey-coloured swimming shorts. Despite all the hours they spend at swimming pools, their skins are usually very pale.

PERVERT AT LOCAL POOL'S TOILET

CHINESE ART DIRECTOR

FAVOURITE PASS TIME
AT TRAFFIC LIGHTS

SHANGHAI COFFEE SHOP ACROBAT

LOADED CHINESE TOWKAY
WITH BAG OF FRUITS

FAT CHINESE BIKER

CHINESE CONTRACTOR
(WORKER)

CHINESE CONTRACTOR
(BOSS)

ART! IS ART! WHAT! IS ART?! IS ART! IS MOVEMENT IN ART? WHAT IS ART? ART IS MOVEMENT. ART IS MOVEMENT IS ART! WHAT IS ART? WHAT IS MOVEMENT IS ART. MOVEMENT IS ART ART IS ART? DANCE IS ART! ART IS EVOLUTION ART IS ART! DANCE! DANCE! DANCE!! ART! ART! DANCE IS MOVEMENT!(IS ART! DANCE IS REVOLUTION ART IS DANCE MOVEMENT MOVEMENTS IS ART!!! DO YOUR OWN THING! IS ART?! OPEN YOUR ((MIND TO THE ENTIRE ART SCENE! NO ONE IS SPARE PEOPLE IS ART! ART IS PEOPLE! LIFE IS ART!! ART! ART! MOVEMENT! ART IS ART! ART! ART!

ART IN LIFE IS ART THERE IS ONE-ONENESS (R!!!! ARTNISM IN ART!!! ART IN REAL LIFE IS ART ART IN REAL LIFE! OO YOU BELIEVE IN MOVEMENT IN ART?! HA! HA! HA! HA! ART! IS ART!! ART IS HA! SOMETHING FLUID! FLUID! ART! ART! ART! FLUID! ART!. FLUID! FLUID! ALI! FLUID! ART IS MOVEMENT! ART IS TRANSPARENT! LIFE IS TRANSPARENT! TRANSPARENCY IS LIFE! ART IS LIFE! LIFE! IS ART! WHAT IS LIFE? LIFE IS MOVEMENT IN ART! HA! HA! HA! HA! MOVE! MOVE! THERE IS ART IN MOVEMENT! YES! ART AND MOVEMENT AND LIFE IS ONE! THERE'S LIFE IN ART AS IN ART LIFE! SO DO YOU WANT TO LIVE? THEN YOU'RE ART! ART! ART! HA! HA! HA!

ART! YE R R ART! MOVEMENT ART! ART! MOVEMENT ART! ART! THER MOVE FLUID! ART!

ART! ART! ART! ART!

EVOLUTION NOT REVOLUTION

ART! ART! ART! ART! DANCE! DANCE! DANCE! ART! DANCE! DANCE! DANCE! ART!

THIS IS BERNARD LO OF MONEY MIND

INVESTMENTS OPPORTUNITIES IN CHINA! THE DOW JONES INDEX LELONG AT PASAR MALAM, SHOULD YOU INVEST? $$! YES!! YES! $$$$$$$$$!! SO SHOULD YOU INVEST? $$$$$! UP OR DOWN! ARE THERE OPPORTUNITIES! WHAT ARE THE RISK INVOLVED? $$$$$$$$! $! $$!! WHAT DO$$ LOCAL INVESTORS THINK!! $$$$$$$$$! $! $!! $$!! GOES PRICES UP OR DOWN!!? $$$! AN ALL TIME HIGH!$$!! WE'LL BE BACK RIGHT AFTER THIS $$$ BREAK! $$$! WELCOME BACK TO MONEY MIND! $$$! ARE THERE OPPORTUNITIES IN CHINA? $$$$ MAKE OR BREAK! INVEST IN FUTURES! BLUE CHIP! $$ WHAT A'BOUT THE TELECOMS SHARES! $$$ SHAPE UP OR SHIP!!OUT! $$ THEY ARE POURING MONEY INTO THAT COUNTRY, SHOULD YOU PLUNGE IN AS WELL? $$$$ CPF INVESTMENT? PUB BILLS? BUS FARES! UP! UP! TELECOM SHARES GROUP A? INVEST!! $$$ BICATERAL RELATIONS ARE OPENING UP! WHAT IS THE FIXED ASSET! COFFEE! INVEST IN COFFEE!! $$$$ $!! THE PE RATIO IS WAY ABOVE! STRIKE PRICE AT 1.34 $$$ SHOULD YOU TAKE IT? BLUE NEXT WEEK CHIPS! WE'LL LOOK CHOCO- AT HOW LATE LOCAL CHIPS! RETAILERS! POTATOE ARE INVESTING CHIPS! IN LOCAL $ INVEST! PORK $$$ IN FARMING!! CHIPS!

DESIRABLE LOCAL MEN NUMBER 3 : FANDI AHMAD

OLE! OLE! OLE! OLE! OLE! NO LAH! PLEASE DON'T DRAW ME! I ONLY PLAY FOOTBALL! OLE! PLAY FOOTBALL ONLY! EVERYBODY PLAY WELL! NO LAH! OLE! DON'T DRAW LAH! NO LAH! I GIVE MY BEST BECAUSE EVERYBODY IT WAS BY LUCK! YEAH! LAH! NO LAH! THE BALL IS ROUND! YES!

OLE! ANYTHING CAN HAPPEN!! OLE! ALL BROKEN LAH! THE OLE! FOOTBALL! MY BONES ARE LAH! BALL IS ROUND! THEY ALL LAH! ARE SO GOOD LAH! NO LAH! OLE! OLE! LAH! DON'T DRAW ME! NO LAH!! OLE! OLE! OLE! OLE!

OLE! OLE! OLE! OLE! OLE! OLE! OLE! OLE! OLE! OLE! OLE! OLE! OLE! OLE! OLE! OLE! NO LAH OLE! OLE! YES! YES! YES! FOOTBALL ALSO OLE! YES! NO LAH! YES! OLE! FOOTBALL IS MY LIFE! OLE! NO LAH! IT WAS ROUND! OLE! BY LUCK! NO LAH OLE! OLE! DON'T GIVE ME OLE! OLE! THE PRIZE, LAH! OLE! OLE! GIVE TO MALEK! OLE! OLE! THE BALL IS OLE! OLE! ROUND! OLE! OLE! NO, DON'T DRAW OLE! OLE! LAH! THE FANS ARE GREAT! THE COACH ALSO SUPER LAH! MALEK, DAVID, ABBAS, STEVEN, MUN HON, KADIR, TONG HAI, JANG JUNG BORHAN! ALL ARE GOOD! TEAMWORK LAH! NO LAH! THE TRAINER LAGI GOOD LAH! THE SPONSORS GOOD LAH! THE BALL IS ROUND! THE BALL IS GOOD LAH! THE BOOTS ALSO GOOD LAH! NO LAH! BY LUCK! NO LAH! NO LAH! NOT ME!

PUMA

Tiger

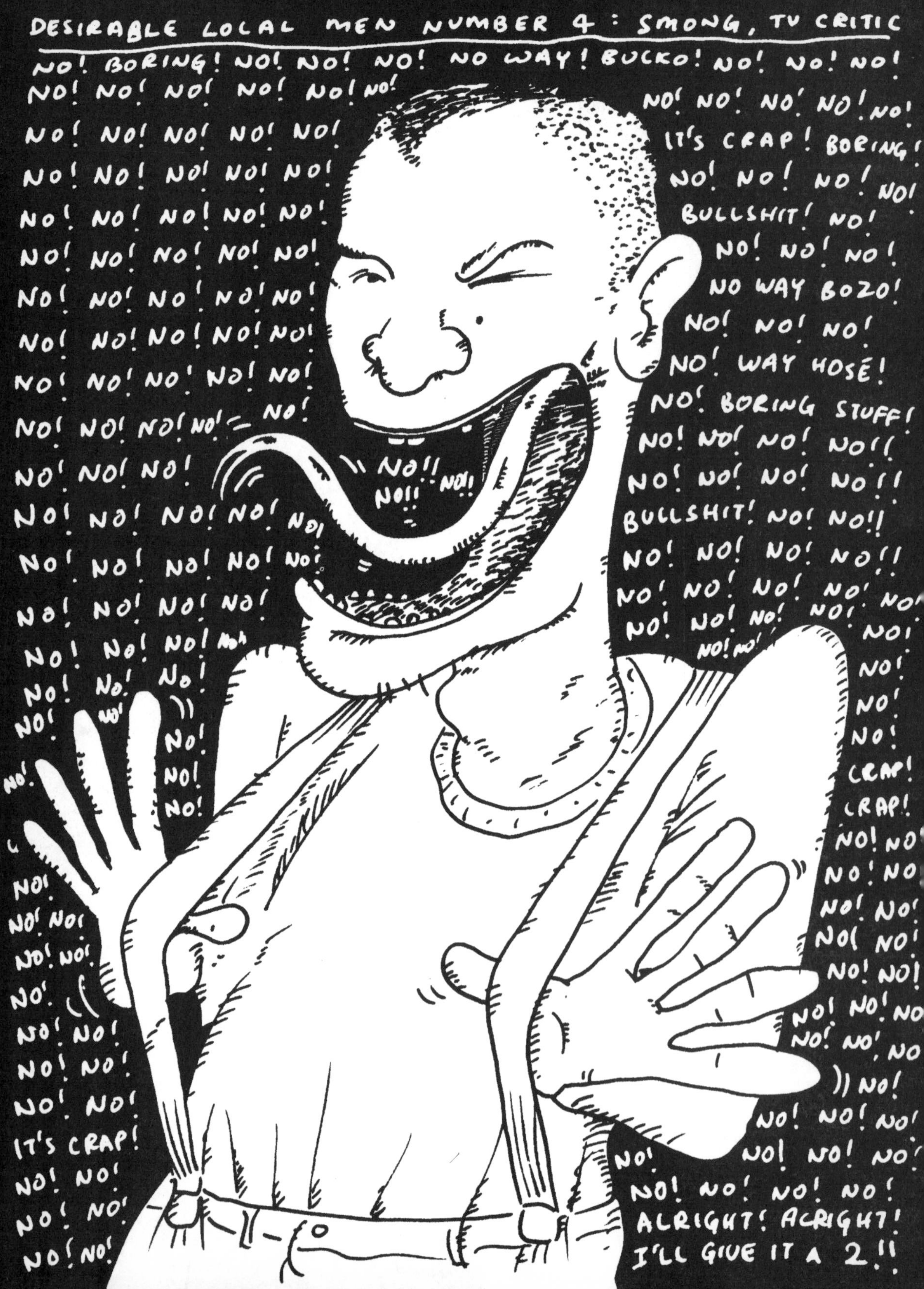

DESIRABLE LOCAL MEN NUMBER 5: JOHNSON LOCK
WHERE IS THE RECIPE FOR YOUR FABULOUS ROAST DUCK?
SECRET! WHERE DO YOU STAY? SECRET!
HOW MUCH DO YOU EARN? SECRET!
HOW MANY STALLS DO YOU HAVE? SECRET!
HOW MANY DUCKS DO YOU SELL A DAY? SECRET!
HOW OLD ARE YOU? SECRET!
ARE YOU MARRIED? SECRET!!
DO YOU HAVE A DRIVING LICENSE? SECRET!!
HOW OLD ARE YOU? SECRET!
DO YOU THINK THE COE WILL GO UP? SECRET!
WHERE DO YOU GO FOR HOLIDAY? SECRET!!
WHAT SPORTS DO YOU PLAY? SECRET!
DO YOU EAT CHICKEN? SECRET!
DO YOU HAVE A PET? SECRET!!
WHAT'S YOUR NAME? SECRET!!!

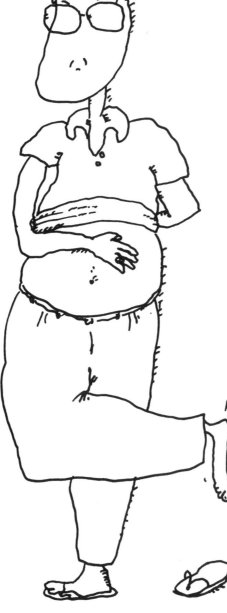

MAN LEANING
AGAINST WALL

If a Singapore woman really appreciates a 'macho' man, she hasn't got to look very far. They are all around her, leaning against walls, scratching their tummies with jade-ringed fingers.

Unlike Caucasian expatriates, the local 'macho' man is very much his own man. He doesn't kow-tow to conventions or fashions. He doesn't set out to impress. He is quite content and self-contained, living his own life according to his own rules.

Occasionally he may cause a few female eyebrows to be raised (or lowered). But at the end of the day, he is a man's man, and women have to take him or leave him as he is.

CHAPTER 7

THE VERY

FEVERISH

FEMINISTS

Feminists believe in women's rights and are opposed to the idea of cruising bars in search of men. Many Singaporean girls are opposed to

DARLING, YOU'RE SO TARTY!

feminists and believe they have every woman's right to go out at night and pick up anybody they wish.

According to many Singaporeans, girls with long black hair are hated by women with short black hair. Perhaps this is because the women with short hair think of themselves as men anyhow, but never get picked up at all.

In fact, some of these women have less hair than the average Caucasian.

There is a popular perception that feminists have little need of refrigerators or airconditioners as they are frigid enough already.

If feminists had their way, there would be no such things as SPGs. There would also be no such things as Australians or New Zealanders.

(76% of New Zealanders believe feminists are actually wolves in sheep's clothing. The other 24% believe feminists are sheep in wolf's clothing, and treat them accordingly.)

The average feminist burns one bra every day. She also burns five copies of this book every day.

Feminists, armed with nothing more than horn-rimmed glasses, are determined to change the face of society in Singapore. By forming a political party called FLAP (Female Liberation Action Party) they will introduce a new series of fines:

Looking at girls in the office FINE $50,

Looking at girls in the office with one hand in your pocket FINE $150,

Looking at girls in the office with one hand in your pocket and the hand appears to be moving FINE $1000,

SCUMBAG *The highest term of respect a Singaporean girl can pay to an Australian businessman at Brannigans.*

QUEUES About the only time expatriate men stand.

HIGHLY-SEXED BLOKE

Any girl wearing spaghetti straps to a bar **FINE $2000**,

Any girl sleeping with a Caucasian with or without her spaghetti straps **FINE $4000**,

Any girl sleeping with a Caucasian with or without her spaghetti straps who also feeds the birds or urinates in the lift on the way to his apartment **FINE $10,000**.

SPAGHETTI STRAP WITH BOLOGNA SAUCE

SOME MORE SPAGHETTI

FOR A MORE SUPERIOR POSITION —
WOMAN ON TOP OF MAN

Feminists take great exception to women being put into categories, especially when men are doing the categorising. And quite rightly so.

However, feminists even take exception to themselves being labelled feminists.

They also disagree with being called liberated women, modern women, independent women, female liberationists, leftist feminists, centrist feminists or rightist feminists.

They also regard the title "Ms" as an insult, because many people think "Ms" is short for "mistake" or "male substitute".

According to feminists, any woman who is critical of other women is an enemy of feminists.

Any woman who self-deprecates is also an enemy of feminists.

Any feminist who uses the term feminist is an enemy of all feminist liberated independent leftist rightist female liberationists.

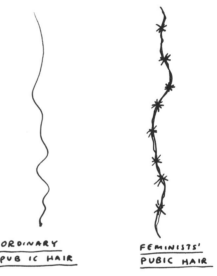

ORDINARY
PUB IC HAIR

FEMINISTS'
PUBIC HAIR

As a result of all this, the average woman is left totally confused about who she is, what she should be called, and what her role in society really is.

THE THREE GREATEST LIES IN THE WORLD:

1.   *"I'll still love you in the morning."*

2.   *"The cheque is in the mail."*

3.   *"I promise I won't do it in your mouth."*

PROMISE Like his youth, something an expatriate male will never keep.

CHAPTER 8

<u>ANG MOHS</u>

<u>AND</u>

<u>MONEY</u>

There is absolutely no truth in the rumour that some local women chase Caucasian men in order to gain money. If money was an objective, they would chase local men.

Apart from which, it would be highly insulting to a Caucasian man to suggest that the bulge in his trousers was caused solely by his wallet. In fact, most Caucasian men manage to keep their wallets exceedingly thin.

95% of all Singaporean women who have been dated by an Australian called John swear that it was not for the money. (His cheap floral ties were offered as proof.)

In fact, it is more likely that Caucasians will go out with the daughters of rich local businessmen in order to gain her family's money.

The daughters of jewellers, stockbrokers, bankers and contractors would be ideal for this purpose.

The benefits for the local businessman would be immense: instead of having a son-in-law called Tan Ah Beng he could introduce a young man from Perth called Fred.

His grandchildren would also have illustrious names like Giles or Stephanie.

Even in the highly refined Jinjang

YOU WANT MY DAUGHTER MARRY YOU?!! OR YOU WANT MARRY MY MONEY?!!

126

area of Kuala Lumpur, the average Joe would be delighted to have an ang moh to help run his timber business.

Caucasians with rich fathers-in-law could enter the family firm and add a certain panache to Chinese dinners.

Any rich tai-tai would love to have an English son-in-law. He could help polish her Nissan NX Coupe and pay her the kind of respect she has sought for a lifetime.

Caucasians in search of money are very adept at social climbing. They are able to rise to the top in Toa Payoh or Kepung virtually without effort.

How can you tell when your daughter is being courted by an avaricious ang moh?

1. When he offers to take your wife to the Chinese opera,
2. When he displays a passionate interest in your

collection of old Hokkien pop
songs,

3.   When he offers to help your wife
clean out your bird cages,

4.   When his shallowness has even
less depth than you thought,

5.   When he offers to sleep with your
wife,

6.   When he offers to sleep with
your mistress, too.

HITCH A RIDE IN SINGAPORE ?! PEACE BROTHER!

But rest assured, if an ang
moh does win your daughter's hand
in marriage, it will only be her hand
that he is interested in. Together,
you and he can look forward to fun
times in the karaoke lounges,
creating havoc and forging a true
East-West partnership whilst
providing mutually beneficial alibis
for each other.

So much for the old myth about ang mohs being milked dry by local girls. Times have changed. As a warning to local girls, here is a list of reasons which an ang moh might give when he asks her for a loan of $200:

1. His bank is closed and he needs to wire cash to his old mum in Milwaukee
2. He needs to send flowers urgently to his uncle in Brisbane who is having a triple-bypass operation ("But last week you told me he died, John." "Well, he's almost dead.")
3. He wants to register a business in their joint names so they can become rich beyond their wildest dreams ("What business, John?" "Dunno, but I'll think of one.")
4. He plans to start a strudel-making factory in Johor Baru
5. He plans to start a second strudel-making factory in Manila
6. He wants to buy a very valuable antique Mercedes-Benz from a tall man called Norman, but first he has to take Norman to lunch
7. He wants to buy the XO Beer concession for Darwin
8. He needs to renew his membership at the Tanglin Club.

MARGIT, Y'KNOW I JUST...COUPLE OF HUNDRED... Y'KNOW ... AW! C'MON !! ... NOT TOO LOUD! I'LL JUST ... LOVE YOU! .... LOVE, LOVE PUSSYCAT! I'LL GIVE YOU SOMETHING SO NICE... (TICKLE! TICKLE!)

BORROWING MONEY - TACTIC NO. 3A

CHAPTER 9

PARTY TIME

WITH THE

ANG MOH

The worst form of party animal is The Buaya.

Ang moh crocodiles have leering smiles that are as false as an SBC newsreader's accent. They look at local girls as though they could make a meal of them. The truth is, the ang moh buaya is himself rather like a meal: a two-day old Big Mac, squashy, limp and highly odorous.

The buaya thinks he can select his victim, close in, and command her to do whatever he wants. In reality, he is a pussycat, a *kucing kurap* to be precise.

Local buaya men can be identified by their white socks. Usually they have enough oil in their hair to hang a Shell sign around their necks. 65% of local buayas have names like Jimmy.

A smaller version of the crocodile is the lounge lizard. 97% are Chinese office equipment salesmen wearing white shoes, who hang around in lounges and bars. 83% have names like Steven or Kenny. They specialise in whispering to girls about the lengths of their organs forgetting, of course, that it's not the size of the sampan that

132

matters, it's the motion in the ocean.

If a local lounge lizard ever got round to holding a party in his **HDB** flat, it would be a mahjong party. Caucasians, on the other hand, approach things differently.

Holding an outrageous party is a popular ang moh method of seduction. Most of the time, however, the parties are outrageously boring and predictable.

Local girls are bemused by the menu of options, all with identical agendas:

The Basic Party: get drunk, get your gear off.

The Fancy Dress Party: get your gear on, get drunk, get your gear off.

The Yacht Party: get seasick, get drunk, get your gear off.

The Pool Party: get drunk, get your gear off before you get wet.

The Wet T-Shirt Party: get drunk, get wet, get your gear off before you catch pneumonia.

If an expatriate lacks the imagination to hold his own party, he can always go to someone else's. In order to pick up local women, he can go to a Sundowners party. Mostly though, he will be too inebriated to pick up anything more than another drink. Because Sundowners parties are usually held at night, there will be inadequate light to see how old these expatriates really are.

At any expatriate party, it is possible to tell a white man's country of origin.

The British will always stand with their legs close together, one hand playing pocket billiards, with both eyes firmly fixed on their reflection in the nearest mirror.

As a tribute to the Australian mining industry, Aussie men will always stand with their legs firmly apart, one hand digging their bottoms at regular five minute intervals.

The French will usually sit, cross-legged, in order to control their bladders.

Americans, on the rare occasions when anybody actually invites them to a party, usually lean against each other for companionship and support.

New Zealanders can be recognised in their fleecy jumpers to remind them of better times at home.

If expatriate wives have been invited, their countries of origin can also be readily determined.

White legs, white teeth, pink noses: British.

Wide legs, wide bottoms, floral dresses: Australian.

Thin legs, thin faces, bored expressions: French.

Stumpy legs, stumpy necks, mega-decibel voices: American.

Plain legs in woollen socks to keep their menfolk interested: New Zealanders.

CHANGI AIRPORT *The nickname for a white expatriate male, because he's usually through in ten minutes.*

EXPAT MACHO TALK AT VELVET UNDERGROUND

CONVERSATIONS FROM A MALE BONDING NIGHT - PT. 1
featuring LARS
C'MON C'MON! GO FOR IT!
YEAH! FOUR KILLERS!!
AW! C'MON! C'MON!
HEARD THIS ONE?!
HA! NO! NO! NO!
YES!! YESRR! HA!
HA! HA!
YO! HA! HA!
YEOLK!! HA!
HA! HA!
MORE! HA!
HA! HA!
YES! NO?
HA! HA!
HA! HA!
YES! HA!
GO FOUR!
IT! HA!
HA! HA!
KISS MY ARSE! HA!
C'MON THE.. HA! HA!
REALLY? HA! HA! HA!
C'MON! C'MON!
OOHH!! HA! HA!
HA! HA! HA!
HA! HA! HA!
HA! HA! HA!
HA! HA! HA! HA! HA! HA!
FOURR KILLERS! HA!
HA! HA! HA! YOU
HA! HA! C'MON!
HA! NOOOO! HA!
HA! IT'S NOTHING!
HA! HA! HA! YO! YO!
C'MON HOMEBOY!! HA!
HA! HA! YES! GULP! HA!
OHH YEAH! FOUR HA!
KILLLLERS! HA! HA!
HA! HA! HA! HA!
HA! OOH! OY!
HA! HA!
HA! HA!
HA! HA!
YEOLP!!
YEOLP!
YEOLP!
OHH!!
HA! HA!
HA! HA!
HA! HA!
LA! LA!
HA! HOI!
HA! HA! HA!
ON! ON! HA! HA!
MASSIVE! HOMEBOY!!
KISS ME ARSE!! HA!
HA! HA! HA! HA!
HA!
HA!
HA! HA!
HA!
HA!
HA! HA!
HA! HA!
HA! HA!
HA!
MY!
Lars
HA!
HA!
AA!!
HA!
HA!!
HA! HA!
C'MON!
HA!
HA!
KE
BEER
HA!
HA!

HA! HA! HA! YEAH! YEAH! HA! HA! HA! HA! HA! HA!
HA! HA! SARONG YEAH! HA! HA! YES THE SARONG!
HA! HA! HA! HA! HA! HA! HA! HA! OOHH! YEAH! HA!
WOAH! HA! HA! MOTHER!! OF SPG!! HA! HA! HA! HA!
OH OH! HA! HA! HA! GOOD LAD! HA! HA! HA! HA! HA!
YES! YES! HA! HA! HA! MMHH HA! PARTY!
HA! HA! GULP!! W GULP! HA! HA! HA!
ANOTHER HA! HA! DRINK! HA! HA!
OOH! YEAH! HA! HA! IT'S SO FUNNY!! HA!
YEP! MOTHER OF SPG! HA! HA! HA! HA!
HA! HA! WHAT ARE YOU? HA! HA! HA!
HA! HA! A WANKER! OOHH! HA! HA! HA!
YEP! YEAP! HA! HA! YES! HA! HA! HA!
OOH!! YES! WHAT! A! WANKER! HA! HA!
LOVELY! LOVELY! HA! AAAA WWANKER!!
CHEERS TO BLOODY THAT!! HA! HA! HA!
HA! HA! HA! HA! GLUP! GLUP! HA! HA!
CHEERS MAN! HA! A WANKER!! HA!
SHIT! SHIT!! HA! HA! HA! HA!
OOHH! HA! SHIT! SHIT! SHIT!
YES! YES! HA! SHIT! SHIT! SHIT!
HA! HA! HA! SHIT! NO SHIT! HA!
HA! HA! HA! NO SHIT! HA! HA!
COOL! SHIT! SHIT! SHIT! ME!
SHIT! SHIT! HA! HA! HA! HA!
SHIT! SHIT! I MET JON AT
SHITTT!!! NEXT PAGE —
WHAT A GUY!!

For many expatriates, every night is party time. And wherever the local trendsetters gather, the ang mohs will surely follow.

For example, when Singapore's most stunning women flock to Fabrice's, they don't flock alone. Sundry expatriates will be on hand to render whatever assistance might be necessary. Fortunately, the music is so good it obscures the sound of their breathless wheezing as they try to keep up with the beat.

There is no truth in the rumour that Fabrice's will soon install a lift, so that exhausted ang mohs don't have to climb the stairs on the way home.

Meanwhile at Velvet Underground, expatriates in velvet underpants cruise the beautiful local scenery. Expatriates find the columns very useful to lean against. After five minutes on the dance floor, they also find the girls very useful to lean against.

No expatriate has ever gone home alone from Velvet Underground; 99.9% have a taxi driver to keep them company.

The handsome young local men who gather at Velvet Underground have no objection whatever to the expatriates being there; it makes them look younger and even more handsome.

Up at Top Ten, there are convenient rails everywhere for elderly expatriates to clutch and lean on. There is also Mama Tequila. When thousands of beautiful women take to the floor, expatriate heart rates jump alarmingly. For this reason, Mama Tequila is now dispensing vitamin pills to every expatriate over the age of 18. (As many weary expatriates have discovered, Mama Tequila will also dispense extra quantities of free salt to counteract dehydration from severe sweating.)

At Number Five in Emerald Hill Road, the name of the bar may soon change to Number Three. This is because most elderly expatriates are comatose after three drinks.

YOGHURT *About the only form of culture to be found in Australia.*

CHAPTER 10

SEX

AND

THE ANG MOH

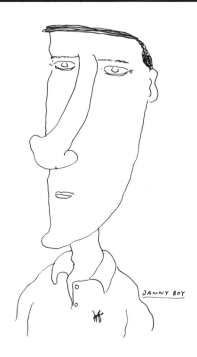

JANNY BOY

The reason why expatriate men are so comfortable with Asian women is because they are of a similar size to inflatable love dolls.

And, after making love to her, the girl will always be let down.

Usually, expatriate love-making techniques are always oral. That is, they're all talk.

Expatriate men begin by enticing local girls to bed with such irresistible invitations as:

1. "Life is short"
2. "The night is but a pup"
3. "Where have you been all my life?"
4. "We owe it to each other"
5. "You don't know what you've been missing"
6. "G'day. Don't s'pose you're on for a quickie?"

Breaking wind is an essential part of expatriate seduction techniques. This is seen (or rather heard) as a sophisticated sign of manhood and maturity. Over 33% of all British expatriates can break wind to the tune of "Rule Britannia". Over 81% of all Australian expatriates can break wind to the tune of "Waltzing Matilda". After a few more drinks and a can of baked beans, they can also break wind to six choruses of "Unchained Melody".

The Worst Case Scenario for a Singaporean girl is being seduced by a large, blubberous expatriate with double chins, wearing socks and sandals and cream shorts that flap in the wind, who possesses a wide general knowledge which sadly excludes how to sexually arouse an Asian woman.

The Worst, Worst Case Scenario is having to spend a weekend on Batam with him.

Singaporean girls are convinced that 85.5% of all expatriate men over the age of 35 are asthmatic. After sex, they are generally wheezing, gasping for air and trembling all over. This is especially surprising because during the act of intercourse she didn't feel a thing.

After a sexual encounter with an Australian expatriate, a Singaporean girl can expect to hear:

1. "Ow wazzat fer yer, zzzzzzzzzzzzzzzz"
2. "Yer wanna do it agin, zzzzzzzzzzzzzzzzzzz"
3. "T'rrific, luv, zzzzzzzzzzzzzzzzzzzzzzzzzzzzzz"
4. "G'night zzzzzzzzzzzzzzzzzzzzzzzzzzzzzzzzzzzzzzzzzzzzzzzz zzzzzzzzzzzzzzzzzzzzzzzzzzzzz".

Many expatriates believe that Singaporean women have periods more

frequently than European women. This is because, week after week, the same women use their periods as an excuse not to go home with him. Some expatriates are also convinced that transvestites have periods, too.

Other expatriates, anticipating a rash of sexual invitations from Singaporean girls, stuff their wallets with condoms. The sad truth is, the wallets are generally the only thing that will be stuffed.

Discos are the favourite pick-up places for expatriates. However, many expatriates would not have been to one in their own home countries for twenty years. If they attempt to dance, they will provide entertainment for the whole crowd.

The second most popular pick-up places for expatriates are disco carparks. Just by opening the door of his flashy sports car, he expects to be flooded with simple-minded Asian girls eager to sleep with him. Usually the only thing he drives home with is his laundry.

THE MAN WHO INVENTED QUICHE.

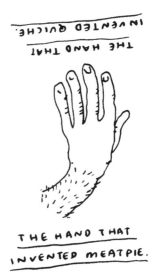

THE HAND THAT INVENTED MEATPIE.

Real men, so Caucasians claim, never eat quiche. Nor do they drink Tequila Sunrise, because it looks 'poofy'.

In fact, to prove how macho they are, Caucasian men go out of their way to pour scorn on homosexuals. Red-blooded Australian men, for example, never refer to homosexuals as gays. They call them queers.

They also call them:

1.   Poofters,
2.   Willy Woofters,
3.   Donut Punchers,
4.   Pillow Biters,
5.   Mattress Munchers,
6.   Bum Burglars.

Many Singaporean girls suspect such aggression is actually a cover for closet gay behaviour.

CLOSET GAY

Ang moh men, on the other hand, deny this — despite the fact they always stick together at parties, ignoring the women, so they can tell their friends about the adventures of their one-eyed trouser snakes. Their folk heroes are men with beer bellies who can do it five times a night. Because they all have beer bellies, and because they all claim to be able to do it five times a night, they are all heroes in their own eyes.

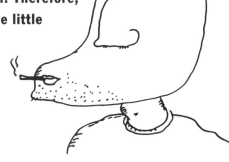

Most expatriate men are very clannish, eating together, drinking together, and going to the loo together. Therefore, they have little knowledge of Singaporean men.

They don't dislike local men; on the contrary, they feel compassionate towards them, never dreaming for a moment that beneath the placid features of Ah Beng lurks a sex monster who can easily do it ten times a night!

LOVE *An emotion which strikes expatriate men whenever they look in a mirror.*

AUZZIE DRAMA QUEEN

LOCAL DRAMA QUEEN

Expatriates believe that Asian girls have been trained for centuries to tell him how handsome he is. Asian girls are far too polite to deny this.

According to theory, the white wedding is supposed to be the dream of every SPG, especially a white wedding to an expatriate. Having been trashed by a long list of ang mohs, the SPG has finally been accepted into the giddy heights of the western world and married her passport out of Singapore.

In reality, she will have acquired the right to live in a lower middle class suburb of London or Sydney, and serve afternoon tea to his parents.

Will the courtship be a thrillingly romantic experience? According to many Singaporean women, that would be about as likely as finding a pharmacy where the pharmacist is actually on duty.

Most Caucasian men consider themselves to be SPGs (Sarong Party Gurus) who can exercise incredible powers over local women. They believe, wrongly, that the average local woman requires little in the way of romance or attention.

However, as the Big Day approaches, he will undergo a curious change.

He will dose himself with steroids in order to perform on the wedding night. His mates from the dragon boat racing team will be there to cheer him on, or at least to help keep him awake.

The wedding reception will continue until the early hours of the morning, to spare the expatriate from as much sexual activity as possible.

After a honeymoon in Bali, where his

girl friends have been strategically booked in to neighbouring hotels, the couple will return to their rented apartment and produce children with upper class names.

The expatriate will revert to his middle class values and start wearing sensible pyjamas to bed.

Other profound changes which his wife will be able to observe:

1. He will become more interested in watching SBC than watching the maid,

A BEAMING EXPAT WITH FAT SPG WIFE ARRIVING IN BALI

All his life, a certain type of white man will remain convinced that he is superior to all other races. And, for that matter, the master of women, Asian or Caucasian. All women, in his eyes, are weak, unintelligent, bimbo-like spendthrifts, requiring his supreme masculinity and sexual stamina to bring a glimmer of glamour into their second-class lives.

Without a white man, he believes, a woman is nothing.

Yet, in fairness to white men, they are a humble lot.

Probably because they have a lot to be humble about.

You see, the Western world is in decline. Like a vast oil tanker drifting out of control, the West is lumbering slowly without purpose towards an uncertain destiny. In contrast, Asia has awakened in a blaze of economic success. In the West, millions of people hunger for the past; in Asia, billions yearn for the future. The next century will be theirs. So for the expatriate in Asia, the phenomenon of an alien culture overtaking his own is a daily reality. And while he can scorn certain Asian attitudes and values, he cannot argue with their viability.

Where once he strode Asian soil as its master, he now walks with uncertainty. At best, he is a trading partner. No more than that. In his mind, he treasures what used to be; and occasionally, in a late-night bar, he can regain some shreds of superiority.

But it is all a transient thing; his presence in Asia is on Asian terms. His own home country will be adrift and at risk, while his Asian base will be a powerhouse of industry and achievement. And should he bother to scratch the surface of even the most affluent, materialistic Asian societies, he will discover centuries-old customs and values firmly in place. Faced with such a bewildering situation, he has two choices: find his own place in the Asian scheme of things, or find a seat on the next plane home.

PENICILLIN *The perfect gift for the Caucasian man who's got everything.*

CHAPTER 12

THE

LAST

WORD

"I believe SPGs don't exist. I also believe that if they do, we don't want to read about them."

— *Decent Housewife, Katong*

"It's bad enough these days if girls wear loose dresses. Why should they have loose morals as well?"

— *Very Decent Housewife, West Coast*

"I would never be seen dead with a Caucasian. Or any other man for that matter. Women can do without those kinds of men."

— *Decent Feminist, Changi*

"Just because they're cheap girls, no one has the right to take cheap shots at them. That's what I say."

— *Lee Boh Chee, Ang Mo Kio*

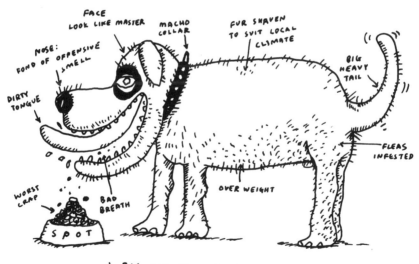

FACE LOOK LIKE MASTER

MACHO COLLAR

FUR SHAVEN TO SVIT LOCAL CLIMATE

NOSE: FOND OF OFFENSIVE SMELL

BIG HEAVY TAIL

DIRTY TONGUE

FLEAS INFESTED

WORST CRAP

BAD BREATH

OVER WEIGHT

SPOT

A BIG DOG IS ONE OF THE STATUS SYMBOL FOR THE EXPATS LIVING HERE. YOU CAN FIND THEM AT LOCAL DOGS SHOWS

allowance of $7,000 and $8,000 and earns an annual salary upwards of $190,500. Armed with this, he manages to turn up at parties with a succulent chocolate bon-bon at his side despite a beer gut and a more-brash-than-dash-manner. Likewise the SPG. She exploits what she has, to get what she wants."

— June Kong, New Paper, September 24, 1994

FINALLY, RECOGNITION FOR THE SPG!

The World Media Says

A generation ago, most books were divided between the English and American markets. Now there are English language presses springing up in Singapore, India and everywhere. Fresh novelists are being introduced by Singapore's FLAME OF THE FOREST...

TIME, in a cover story, 'The Empire Writes Back' by Pico Iyer

FLAME OF THE FOREST has shown a flair for publishing bestsellers...

THE ASIAN WALL STREET JOURNAL

FLAME OF THE FOREST has established itself as a leading publisher of popular paperbacks.

THE STAR

Angsana Books
AN IMPRINT OF FLAME OF THE FOREST